GLOBAL VIEWPOINTS

The War on Terror

Other Books of Related Interest:

At Issue Series
Rebuilding the World Trade Center

Current Controveries Series
Islamophobia
The Middle East

Introducing Issues with Opposing Viewpoints Series
Islam
Terrorism

Issues That Concern You Series
War

Opposing Viewpoints Series
Bioterrorism

GLOBALVIEWPOINTS

I The War on Terror

Noah Berlatsky, Book Editor

GREENHAVEN PRESS
A part of Gale, Cengage Learning

GALE
CENGAGE Learning·

Detroit • New York • San Francisco • New Haven, Conn • Waterville, Maine • London

Elizabeth Des Chenes, *Director, Publishing Solutions*

© 2012 Greenhaven Press, a part of Gale, Cengage Learning

Gale and Greenhaven Press are registered trademarks used herein under license.

For more information, contact:
Greenhaven Press
27500 Drake Rd.
Farmington Hills, MI 48331-3535
Or you can visit our Internet site at gale.cengage.com

LIBRARY OF CONGRESS CATALOGING-IN-PUBLICATION DATA

The war on terror / Noah Berlatsky, book editor.
   p. cm. -- (Global viewpoints)
   Includes bibliographical references and index.
   ISBN 978-0-7377-6271-6 (hbk.) -- ISBN 978-0-7377-6447-5 (pbk.)
   1. Terrorism--Prevention--Juvenile literature. 2. Terrorism--Juvenile literature.
   3. War on Terrorism, 2001-2009--Juvenile literature. I. Berlatsky, Noah.
   HV6431.W3592 2012
   363.325--dc23
                                                          2012008665

Printed in Mexico
2 3 4 5 6 7 16 15 14 13 12

Contents

Foreword   11

Introduction   14

Chapter 1: The Causes of Terrorism

1. The **United States** Should Fight Global   20
   Poverty to Reduce Terrorism
   Holly Ramer
   Poverty fuels violence and terrorist attacks on the United
   States. Therefore, a global campaign against poverty
   would help US security interests in the War on Terror.

2. Failed States Like **Somalia** and **Pakistan**   24
   Cause Terrorism
   Max Boot
   Failed states such as Somalia and parts of Pakistan breed
   terrorism, piracy, and lawlessness. To fight these ills, the
   international community should put failed states under
   international administration.

3. Failed States Like **Somalia** Do Not   30
   Cause Terrorism
   Paul D. Williams
   Failed states like Somalia are too chaotic to be effective
   bases for terrorism. Therefore, the focus on failed states
   in the War on Terror is flawed.

4. Worldwide, the Islamic Religion Is the Cause   37
   of Terrorism
   Daniel Greenfield
   The Koran and Islam advocate violence. The basic violence of Islam is the cause of Islamic terrorism, not poverty, political alienation, or historical injustice.

5. In **Latin America**, Islam Is Not Linked   43
   to Terrorism
   Vitória Peres de Oliveira
   In Latin America, Muslim communities are integrated
   into the population and often are relatively well-off.
   These communities have little interest in promoting terrorism.

Chapter 2: Human Rights and the War on Terror

1. In **Britain**, Respect for Human Rights Helps   53
in the War on Terror
Lord Phillips of Worth Matravers
Through the Human Rights Act, the British courts uphold the rights of terrorism suspects, including immigrants threatened with deportation. The adherence to
human rights reduces resentment and supports society; it
is a crucial weapon in the War on Terror.

2. **Europe**'s Misguided Focus on Human Rights   66
Has Hampered the US War on Terror
Sally McNamara
The European Union's focus on human rights and its
condemnation of US detention and antiterrorism policies
has hurt US efforts to fight the War on Terror.

3. **China** Uses the War on Terror to Repress   78
Uighur Separatist Movements
Chien-peng Chung
China characterizes its opposition to Muslim Uighur
separatist movements as part of the War on Terror. By
doing so, China makes repression and human rights violations more palatable to both domestic and international audiences.

4. The **US** War on Terror Should Be Fought with   84
Intelligence, Not Military Force
Sara Daly
Although the US military could crush the enemy, the ter-
rorist threat in the United States should be left to the po-
lice who can monitor the activities of local extremists.

5. In **Afghanistan** and **Pakistan**, Improving   89
Women's Rights Helps in the War on Terror
Charles M. Sennott

Women in Afghanistan and Pakistan often work for peace and against terrorist indoctrination. Giving women authority and a voice in the community helps to reduce violence and terror.

Periodical and Internet Sources Bibliography 94

Chapter 3: Government Responses to Terrorist Attacks

1. Like **Norway**, the **United Kingdom** Should 96
Learn to React Calmly to Terrorist Attacks
Iain Macwhirter

Norway reacted with calm and unity to a deadly terrorist attack. The United Kingdom's reaction to terrorist attacks has been less measured. It should learn from Norway.

2. **Russia** Struggles to Find the Correct Response 102
to Terror Attacks
Sergei Roy

Following terrorist attacks, Russians reacted with anger and officials called for severe security measures. The actual government response, however, was more measured.

3. **Germany** May Institute Full-Body Scanners in 106
Airports in Response to a Terrorist Attack
Spiegel

After a foiled terrorist attack, Germany is considering digital strip search scanners in airports, despite some ongoing privacy concerns.

4. **India**'s Response to Terrorism Has Been 113
Complex and Effective
Ajit Doval

India has used its democratic institutions and a focus on policing rather than military solutions to craft an effective counterterrorism program.

5. **India**'s Response to Terrorism Has 120
Been Ineffectual
Ajai Sahni

India has failed to craft theoretical or practical responses to terrorism, and its policing and security apparatus is deeply ineffectual in dealing with terrorist threats.

6. **Israeli-Palestinian** Peace Negotiations Must   130
Not Be Derailed by Terrorist Attacks
Matthew Levitt
For Israeli-Palestinian peace negotiations to be successful,
both parties must be prepared to press on toward peace,
despite efforts by terrorists to derail talks. Anticipating
responses to terrorist attacks before negotiations begin is
vital.

Periodical and Internet Sources Bibliography   139

Chapter 4: The Future of the War on Terror

1. In **Afghanistan**, the Death of Osama bin Laden   141
Must Not End the War on Terror
Abbas Daiyar
Osama bin Laden's death is an important symbolic victory, but the threats of al Qaeda and the Taliban are not
over. Pakistanis, Afghans, and the United States must
press forward in the War on Terror.

2. Declare Victory and End the 'Global War   148
on Terror'
Gideon Rachman
The death of Osama bin Laden is a good moment for
the United States to end the War on Terror. The threat of
terrorism has been hyped, and the United States needs to
decrease the time and money spent on intelligence gathering.

3. **Pakistanis** Fear Economic Isolation   153
Daily Star
After the discovery and death of Osama bin Laden in Pakistan, Pakistan fears that Washington might use its influence over financial institutions to harm the Pakistani
economy.

4. The West Must Do More to End the Injustice   157
That Motivates Jihad
Zia Haq
Osama bin Laden's death will not end global jihad. The
jihad can only be ended when its causes in global injus-
tice and frustration are addressed.

5. The Muslim World Must Do More   162
   to Reject Jihad
   Abdullah Iskandar

   Muslims need to condemn Osama bin Laden's violence
   more thoroughly and consistently, and they must not
   glorify his memory.

6. In the West, Osama bin Laden's Death Should   166
   Not Be an Excuse for Racism or Hate
   Ray Hanania

   Osama bin Laden's death provoked celebrations of violence and anti-Muslim rhetoric. Israel and the West must
   not demonize Islam and should instead strive for peace
   and understanding.

Periodical and Internet Sources Bibliography   171

For Further Discussion   172

Organizations to Contact   174

Bibliography of Books   179

Index   182

Foreword

"The problems of all of humanity can only be solved by all of humanity."
— Swiss author Friedrich Dürrenmatt

Global interdependence has become an undeniable reality. Mass media and technology have increased worldwide access to information and created a society of global citizens. Understanding and navigating this global community is a challenge, requiring a high degree of information literacy and a new level of learning sophistication.

Building on the success of its flagship series, Opposing Viewpoints, Greenhaven Press has created the Global Viewpoints series to examine a broad range of current, often controversial topics of worldwide importance from a variety of international perspectives. Providing students and other readers with the information they need to explore global connections and think critically about worldwide implications, each Global Viewpoints volume offers a panoramic view of a topic of widespread significance.

Drugs, famine, immigration—a broad, international treatment is essential to do justice to social, environmental, health, and political issues such as these. Junior high, high school, and early college students, as well as general readers, can all use Global Viewpoints anthologies to discern the complexities relating to each issue. Readers will be able to examine unique national perspectives while, at the same time, appreciating the interconnectedness that global priorities bring to all nations and cultures.

Material in each volume is selected from a diverse range of sources, including journals, magazines, newspapers, nonfiction books, speeches, government documents, pamphlets, organization newsletters, and position papers. Global Viewpoints is truly global, with material drawn primarily from international sources available in English and secondarily from US sources with extensive international coverage.

Features of each volume in the Global Viewpoints series include:

- An **annotated table of contents** that provides a brief summary of each essay in the volume, including the name of the country or area covered in the essay.

- An **introduction** specific to the volume topic.

- A **world map** to help readers locate the countries or areas covered in the essays.

- For each viewpoint, an **introduction** that contains notes about the author and source of the viewpoint explains why material from the specific country is being presented, summarizes the main points of the viewpoint, and offers three **guided reading questions** to aid in understanding and comprehension.

- **For further discussion** questions that promote critical thinking by asking the reader to compare and contrast aspects of the viewpoints or draw conclusions about perspectives and arguments.

- A worldwide list of **organizations to contact** for readers seeking additional information.

- A **periodical bibliography** for each chapter and a **bibliography of books** on the volume topic to aid in further research.

- A comprehensive **subject index** to offer access to people, places, events, and subjects cited in the text, with the countries covered in the viewpoints highlighted.

Global Viewpoints is designed for a broad spectrum of readers who want to learn more about current events, history, political science, government, international relations, economics, environmental science, world cultures, and sociology—students doing research for class assignments or debates, teachers and faculty seeking to supplement course materials, and others wanting to understand current issues better. By presenting how people in various countries perceive the root causes, current consequences, and proposed solutions to worldwide challenges, Global Viewpoints volumes offer readers opportunities to enhance their global awareness and their knowledge of cultures worldwide.

Introduction

> *"Terrorism continues to pose a serious security challenge to Australia. The Australian government remains resolute in its commitment to protect Australia, its people and interests from this threat."*
>
> —Kevin Rudd,
> *former prime minister of Australia,*
> *Foreword to "Counter-Terrorism*
> *White Paper: Securing Australia,*
> *Protecting Our Community," 2010*

Australia is an island located—literally—on the other side of the world from the United States. Despite its distance from America, however, Australia was deeply affected by the September 11, 2001, attacks on the United States and the subsequent War on Terror. In fact, according to a September 10, 2011, article in the *New Zealand Herald*, "Since September 11, 2001, more Australian civilians have been killed in terrorist acts than Americans."

Australia sent around fifteen hundred troops to join the US operation in Afghanistan against the terrorist group al Qaeda shortly after the September 11 attacks. Australia also provided a force of around five hundred troops to aid in the war in Iraq, which was presented by the United States as part of its War on Terror. No Australian military casualties occurred in Iraq, and all troops were pulled from the country in 2009. However, Australia's participation in the Afghan war continues as of early 2012. In Afghanistan, Australian forces have sustained thirty-two casualties, and 213 soldiers have been wounded, according to information on the website of the Australian Department of Defence.

Besides the military actions in Iraq and Afghanistan, Australia had its own major encounter with terror against civilians on October 12, 2002, when three bombs were detonated in a tourist district on the Indonesian island of Bali. Of the 202 people killed, 88 were Australians. Four more Australians were killed in terror attacks in the same location in 2005, as reported by the *New Zealand Herald*.

Both Australia's participation in the War on Terror and the way in which the war has been conducted have been controversial. Australian actress Cate Blanchett, for example, spoke out against Australian participation in the war in Iraq, saying that "our blind allegiance to the United States is embarrassing," as quoted by Monica Attard on the November 11, 2007, broadcast of *Sunday Profile*. Along the same lines, Mark Latham, in a February 26, 2003, column at *On Line Opinion*, criticized the then Australian prime minister John Howard for sending troops to Iraq when "the Bali bombers are yet to be brought to justice." He added:

> The government has just spent $15 million on advertising to warn Australians of the terrorist threat in this country. But if, as the government argues, our nation is under threat, then we should not be sending our best troops and equipment to the other side of the world. If terrorists were to take control of an international hotel in a major Australian city, where would we want our SAS [Special Air Service] and commando troops to be?

In addition to the war in Iraq, the War on Terror in general has faced significant public skepticism in Australia, according to poll results reported by Dan Oakes in a June 3, 2011, article in the *Age*. Oakes said that two-thirds of Australians thought the War on Terror would never end, while only 4 percent surveyed thought that terrorism was the most important problem facing the nation. In addition, a full 31 percent of Australians thought that American policy had provoked the September 11, 2001, attacks.

On the other hand, many commentators and politicians in Australia have argued that the War on Terror is vital for Australia's national security. For example, on October 9, 2001, shortly after the September 11 attacks, Darryl S.L. Jarvis of the University of Sydney argued that terrorism damaged the community of nations and, therefore, was directly antithetical to Australian interest. "Well we might ponder the rectitude of the foreign policy of the United States," he said, "but we must not fail to meet terrorist violence with force, save the very structures of the international system will be imperilled."

In defending Australia's commitment to Iraq several years later, Alexander Downer, Liberal Party politician and former minister for foreign affairs, made similar points. He argued in an April 13, 2004, speech to the National Press Club that

> There are some who believe that the war against terror is something that we can avoid . . . that we can roll into a ball and, in the false security of an inward gaze, behave like we are a small target . . . and leave others to fight our battles. These people are wrong.
>
> We need to be ever-cognisant of the reality—terrorism is a threat today that knows no geographic boundaries and no moral boundaries.

On September 12, 2011, the tenth anniversary of the September 11, 2001, attacks on the United States, Kevin Rudd, the Australian minister for foreign affairs (and former prime minister), reaffirmed Australia's commitment to the War on Terror. "We must never shirk the tough task of standing up to terrorism, and never avoid paying the price to thwart it," he insisted.

In line with this sentiment, Australia's prime minister, Julia Gillard, has refused to set a deadline for withdrawing all troops from Afghanistan, despite strong criticism from Parliament. Green member of Parliament Adam Bandt, for example, insisted that an open-ended commitment in Afghanistan "goes completely against the will of the Australian people," as quoted by Greg Ansley in a November 22, 2011, article in the *New Zealand Herald*. In contrast, Gillard insisted that "Australians well understand that days of progress and days of sorrow still lie ahead" in Afghanistan.

The remainder of this book will look at other issues and controversies involving the War on Terror. Chapters include The Causes of Terrorism, Human Rights and the War on Terror, Government Responses to Terrorist Attacks, and The Future of the War on Terror. Like Australia, countries throughout the world have been affected by terrorism and have struggled to decide how best to respond to it.

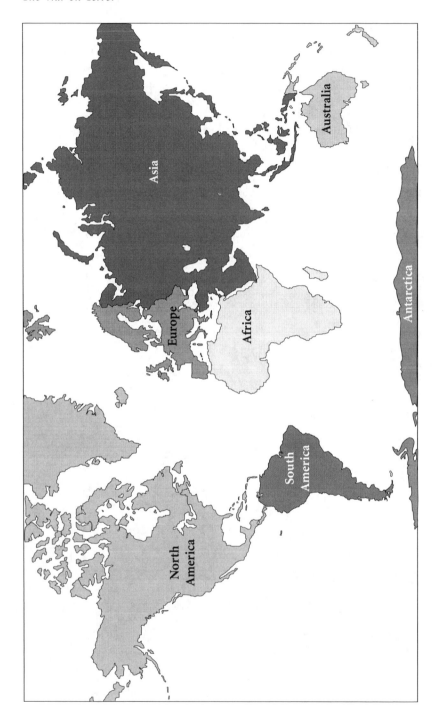

GLOBALVIEWPOINTS

CHAPTER 1

The Causes of Terrorism

The United States Should Fight Global Poverty to Reduce Terrorism

Holly Ramer

Holly Ramer is a writer for the Associated Press. In the following viewpoint, she reports on US presidential candidate John Edwards's views on poverty and terrorism when he was campaigning for the Democratic nomination in 2007. Edwards argues that poverty fuels violence and terrorist attacks on the United States. He says that a global campaign against poverty would help US security interests in the War on Terror. Edwards also advocates an attack on poverty in the United States that he says would make the US workforce stronger.

As you read, consider the following questions:

1. Edwards calls for spending $3 billion a year on what program?
2. What position has Edwards not titled, according to this viewpoint?
3. What are some of Edwards's proposed solutions for eliminating poverty in the United States within thirty years?

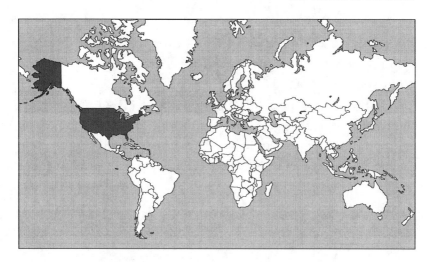

Democratic presidential hopeful John Edwards on Thursday [March 15, 2007] outlined what he called "an audacious plan" to tackle global poverty that includes educating 23 million children in poor countries and creating a cabinet-level position to oversee other initiatives.

Poverty and National Security

Seeking to link poverty in other countries to the United States' national security, Edwards argued that militant extremists in nations torn apart by poverty and civil war have replaced government educational systems and are teaching young people to hate the United States.

"When you understand that, it suddenly becomes clear: Global poverty is not just a moral issue for the United States—it is a national security issue for the United States," he said at Saint Anselm College.

"If we tackle it, we have the chance to change a generation of potential extremists and enemies into a generation of friends," Edwards said.

Edwards called for spending $3 billion a year to extend primary education to millions of children in developing countries. Combating terrorism should begin in classrooms, not battlefields, he said.

His plan also includes $600 million a year for health care initiatives, including a worldwide summit on clean drinking water and sanitation and a sixfold increase in funding for clean water programs.

Getting to the root of global poverty will require increasing both political and economic opportunities for the poor, he said, at a cost of about $1.4 billion. And it will require one person to oversee those efforts, he said.

Cabinet rank has been given to the heads of the Environmental Protection Agency, the Office of Management and Budget, the national drug czar and the U.S. trade representative.

Eliminating Waste and Attacking Poverty

In a conference call before the speech, Edwards told reporters he hasn't titled the cabinet-level post, but noted that more than 50 U.S. agencies work on international assistance.

"Our current effort has plenty of bureaucracy—what a surprise," he said. "What our system lacks is efficiency and accountability. As president, I intend to change that."

Edwards said details of how he would pay for the $5 billion plan would come later, but said he would not propose raising taxes for middle-class taxpayers.

"Don't think for a second that addressing poverty is charity—addressing it makes our workforce stronger."

"If, and I'm not saying at this moment I'm going to do it, but if there has to be another revenue source, it can't come from middle- or low-income taxpayers," he said.

Edwards has acknowledged that a key component of his plan to end domestic poverty—providing universal health care—will require raising taxes. He proposes rolling back President [George W.] Bush's tax cuts for people who earn more than $200,000 and having the government collect back taxes to raise money for health coverage.

Edwards, who established a research center on poverty after his failed 2004 campaign [for president], has set a goal of eliminating poverty in the United States in 30 years. His proposed solutions include creating a million temporary jobs for low-income workers, strengthening labor laws, increasing tax credits for working families and making housing and higher education more affordable.

"Don't think for a second that addressing poverty is charity—addressing it makes our workforce stronger," he said. "If we build a working society, we won't just try the old solutions and the old politics. Instead we will work as a national community to change fundamentally the culture of poverty itself and create the conditions . . . [for] all people to lift themselves up into the middle class."

Accomplishing those goals will require a different approach to politics, Edwards said, criticizing the Bush administration for ignoring the will of the public.

"We can no longer accept having the course of our country dictated by a relatively few people who push onto the rest of us policies that suit their particular interests," he said.

He didn't spare his own party from criticism, either, saying it's time to abandon a path "where the Senate passes nonbinding resolutions about the war in Iraq [begun in 2003] while the war escalates."

Failed States Like Somalia and Pakistan Cause Terrorism

Max Boot

Max Boot is a senior fellow at the Council on Foreign Relations and the author of War Made New: Technology, Warfare, and the Course of History, 1500 to Today. *In the following viewpoint, he argues that failed states such as Somalia and parts of Pakistan breed terrorism, piracy, and lawlessness. He says that to fight these ills, the international community should put failed states under international administration. Unfortunately, he says, international forces and organizations are unwilling to take the necessary steps to impose order. Until they are, Boot recommends limited military responses but doubts that these will eliminate terrorism or piracy.*

As you read, consider the following questions:

1. In what parts of Pakistan does Boot say terrorist groups have established a state within a state?
2. What does Boot say was the solution to lawlessness in troubled lands in the nineteenth century?
3. What are the second-best alternatives Boot discusses as possible responses to piracy and terrorism?

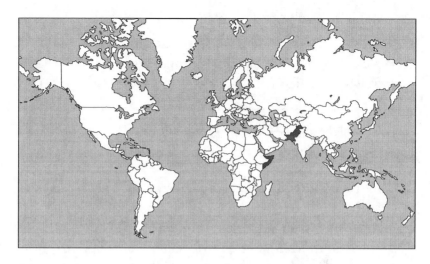

Ever since the end of the Cold War, there has been much chatter about the problem of failed states. Now we are seeing some of the terrible consequences of state failure on the periphery of the broader Middle East.

Terrorism and Piracy

In Pakistan, terrorist groups such as the Taliban, al Qaeda, and Lashkar-e-Taiba have established themselves as a state within a state. They have virtual free rein in the Federally Administered Tribal Areas [a semiautonomous area in northwestern Pakistan] and a lesser but still substantial amount of leeway in the North-West Frontier [Province] and other provinces. That makes it all too easy for them to launch attacks such as those that killed more than 170 people in Mumbai [India]. Or other attacks that kill NATO [North Atlantic Treaty Organization] soldiers in Afghanistan [where NATO troops are fighting a war].

Across the Indian Ocean, pirates are terrorizing passing ships. The International Maritime Bureau reports that 92 ships have been attacked and 36 hijacked this year off the coast of Somalia and Yemen. At least 14 ships and 260 crew members are being held hostage. A passenger liner with more than 1,000 people aboard barely avoided being the pirates' latest prize. Vessels that were not so lucky include a Saudi oil tanker carrying two million barrels of crude oil and a Ukrainian freighter loaded with tanks and other weapons.

The essential problem in both Somalia and Pakistan is a failure of governance.

The predations of pirates and terrorists—two species of international outlaws—have caused much hand-wringing and a so-far unsuccessful search for solutions. The United Nations [U.N.] has authorized warships to enter Somalia's territorial waters and use "all necessary force" against the pirates. A number of states, including the U.S., have sent their own naval vessels to help, but their numbers are grossly inadequate to safeguard thousands of miles of water. The increasingly bold desperados are venturing farther and farther from shore in search of ever more lucrative prizes.

The response in Pakistan has been just as limited and just as ineffective. India, the U.S., Afghanistan and other concerned states have spent years begging Islamabad [capital of Pakistan] to crack down on terrorists. These pleas have been backed up by offers of aid and threats if inaction continues. Neither has done much good. The Pakistani army appears either unwilling or unable—maybe both—to take effective action against powerful jihadist groups that have long-standing links with its own Inter-Services Intelligence agency. In desperation, the U.S. has resorted to picking off individual terrorists with unmanned aerial vehicles. This tactic works and should be continued, but it is no more than a Band-Aid on a gaping wound.

The Rule of Law

The essential problem in both Somalia and Pakistan is a failure of governance. The question is: What if anything can out-

Pakistan as a Failed State

Several factors have led to Pakistan becoming a failed state. After decades of coups and interfighting, Pakistan's government has become weak and fractured. Because the government is so weak, it is incapable of dealing with Pakistan's greatest problems, such as attacks by the Taliban [a militant Islamic Afghan group] in the northern regions of the country. The government is also unable to adequately care for Pakistan's sizable refugee population, which consists of people who have fled conflicts with the Taliban and people who were displaced from their homes by earthquakes.

Matthew Bukovac, Failed States: Unstable Countries in the 21st Century. *New York: Rosen Publishing Group, 2011, p. 22.*

side powers do to bring the rule of law to these troubled lands? In the 19th century, the answer was simple: European imperialists would plant their flag and impose their laws at gunpoint. The territory that now comprises Pakistan was not entirely peaceful when it was under British rule. Nor was Somalia under Italian and British sovereignty. But they were considerably better off than they are today—not only from the standpoint of Western countries but also from the standpoint of their own citizens.

You might think that such imperialism is simply unacceptable today. But you would be only partially right. There have been a number of instances in recent years of imperialism-in-all-but-name. Bosnia and Kosovo [two states in eastern Europe where NATO intervened to end ethnic violence in the 1990s]—still wards of NATO and the European Union [as of 2008]—are prominent examples of how successful such interventions can be in the right circumstances.

The real difficulty with emulating these examples is not a lack of legitimacy. That can always be conferred by the United Nations or some other multilateral organization. Harder to overcome is a lack of will. Ragtag guerrillas have proven dismayingly successful in driving out or neutering international peacekeeping forces. Think of American and French troops blown up in Beirut in 1983 [when truck bombs struck military barracks killing 299], or the "Black Hawk Down" incident in Somalia in 1993 [in which 19 American soldiers were killed].

Too often, when outside states do agree to send troops, they are so fearful of casualties that they impose rules of engagement that preclude meaningful action. Think of the ineffectiveness of African Union peacekeepers dealing with genocide in Darfur today or of U.N. peacekeepers dealing with genocide in Rwanda in 1994. Even the world's mightiest military alliance is not immune from these problems. Witness the problems NATO has encountered in trying to get member states to live up to their commitments in Afghanistan.

Until we are willing to place more ungoverned spaces under international administration, evils such as piracy and terrorism will continue to flourish.

A Failure of Will

If NATO won't do enough to win the war in Afghanistan, its highest priority, there is scant chance that it will commit troops to police Pakistan's tribal areas or Somalia's coast. And if NATO members won't act, who will? That difficulty renders moot ideas such as the one just put forward by foreign-policy theorist Robert Kagan: "Have the international community declare that parts of Pakistan have become ungovernable and a menace to international security. Establish an international force to work with the Pakistanis to root out terrorist camps in Kashmir as well as in the tribal areas."

It is a tragedy that such proposals have no chance of being acted upon until some truly great tragedy occurs. If we suffer another 9/11 [referring to the September 11, 2001, terrorist attacks on the United States] or worse and the culprits can be traced to Pakistan, then the U.S. and its allies would summon the wherewithal to act. But not until then.

Given that dismal reality, it makes sense to think of second-best alternatives. In the case of the Somali pirates, creative solutions can include using air and naval power to hit the bases from which they operate, and employing Blackwater [a private military consulting firm] and other mercenaries to add their protective efforts to those of the world's navies. In Pakistan that means continuing air strikes and providing assistance to tribal militias which have their own grievances against jihadist interlopers. In both places, the U.S. should be doing what it can, in cooperation with allies and multilateral organizations, to bolster central authority.

But we should not fool ourselves into thinking that any of these measures has much chance of success. Until we are willing to place more ungoverned spaces under international administration, evils such as piracy and terrorism will continue to flourish.

Failed States Like Somalia Do Not Cause Terrorism

Paul D. Williams

Paul D. Williams is an associate professor in international security at the University of Warwick in the United Kingdom. In the following viewpoint, Williams argues that failed states like Somalia are too chaotic to be effective bases for terrorism. International peacekeepers, he says, can violate the sovereignty of failed states and attack terrorists directly. In addition, Williams argues, terrorists in failed states often become targets of rival factions. For these reasons, he says, terrorists prefer to operate in weak states rather than failed ones. Williams concludes that the Western focus on failed states in the War on Terror is flawed.

As you read, consider the following questions:

1. What does Williams say was al Qaeda's original primary purpose?
2. According to Williams, what is distinctive about al Qaeda's organizational form?
3. Failed states are inhospitable to foreigners, according to Williams. Why is this a problem for terrorist organizations?

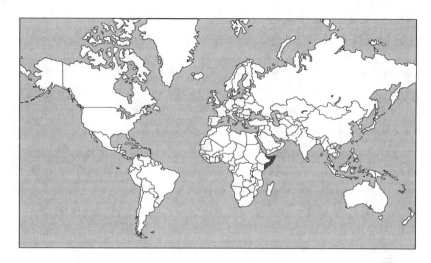

As the QDR [that is, the 2006 U.S. Department of Defense Quadrennial Defense Review] made clear, 'The enemies in this war are not traditional conventional military forces but rather dispersed, global terrorist networks that exploit Islam to advance radical political aims'. Public enemy No. 1 was [the international terrorist organization] al-Qa'ida . . . , which according to Washington operated in over 80 countries. Al-Qa'ida had been forged in the crucible of Afghanistan's wars but was first and foremost a movement that developed around Arab Sunni [an Islamic denomination] radicals with the primary purpose of assuming power in the Arab states, especially Saudi Arabia. In this sense, it is important to recall that despite much of the rhetoric (from Western governments and the movements themselves) describing international terrorism as a global phenomenon, in many respects 'Islamist movements were primarily caused by, and directed at, conditions *within* their own societies' [according to F. Halliday.] This is not to deny al-Qa'ida's evident desire to kill infidels wherever they might be found, but merely to point out the regionally specific origins and primary goals of America's principal enemy. This is important to bear in mind when searching for ways to bring the long war to an end.

Al-Qa'ida vs. Other Terrorist Organizations

In organizational terms, al-Qa'ida is distinct from most other terrorist organizations in four main respects. First, its organizational form is fluid. Since the 9/11 attacks [referring to the September 11, 2001, terrorist attacks on the United States] it has come to be thought of as representing both a global jihadist movement consisting of *ad hoc* cells linked together via the virtual sanctuary of the Internet as well as a label for a broader umbrella group of independent entities that share some ideological assumptions and are willing to cooperate over certain issues. Second, al-Qa'ida's method of recruitment is distinct from its predecessors. In this respect it is more akin to a social movement than a terrorist organization, often attracting followers to join its ranks voluntarily rather than recruiting them into service. Nevertheless, as [A.K.] Cronin notes, exposure to al-Qa'ida's ideology alone has not been sufficient to attract recruits—as its failure to attract many members in either Sudan or Afghanistan suggests. Rather, evidence from al-Qa'ida's operatives suggests that links of friendship and kinship facilitated by a 'bridging person' have been crucial. This method of recruitment has worked particularly well in the Maghreb [Northwest Africa] and Southeast Asia. Third, al-Qa'ida's means of supporting its activities are novel in several respects. The relatively small amounts of money required to launch its attacks have come from diverse sources including charitable donations, petty crime and fraud. It has also extracted funds from a wide range of businesses related to the organization—at one point, [al-Qa'ida leader Osama] bin Laden was estimated to own around 80 companies worldwide. Finally, al-Qa'ida has successfully harnessed the revolution in information technology to carry out its communication through such mechanisms as mobile phones, text messaging, instant messaging, e-mail, Internet chat rooms and blogs. It has even managed to assemble its own virtual training manual; the so-called 'The Encyclopedia of Jihad'.

Inhospitable to Terrorism

Several scholars and analysts have cast doubts on the idea that failed states offer the right environment for terrorists. Ken Ross, Beth Greener-Barcham and Manuhuia Barcham, Ken Menkhaus and Stewart Patrick ... have all expressed reservations about the premise that failed states breed terrorism. Commenting on the Pacific Islands, Ross observes that this type of argument simply reprises Cold War concerns that weak states in the region would make them vulnerable to communism. 'It is a seriously misjudged perspective', he says, 'for these [Pacific Island] states lack the necessary oxygen for would-be terrorists, for whom the concept "terror is theatre" is all important. This region lacks the facilities'. Greener-Barcham and Barcham express the same doubts about the 'failed states-terrorism connection' in the South Pacific, arguing that 'the possibilities for terrorist activity are arguably lessened in the Pacific as it is characterized by a lack of land borders and soft targets, and by small-scale closely knit and predominantly rural societies where everybody knows everyone else's business. Menkhaus offers a similar assessment: 'In fact, transnational criminals and terrorists have found zones of complete state collapse like Somalia to be relatively inhospitable territory out of which to operate'. And so too does Patrick. . . . As he explains, 'not all weak and failed states are afflicted by terrorism', nor is the terrorism that may arise there necessarily transnational. These analysts dispute the contention that failing or failed states are hotbeds of terrorism.

Richard Devetak, "Failures, Rogues and Terrorists:
States of Exception and the North/South Divide,"
in Security and the War on Terror, *ed. Alex J. Bellamy,*
Roland Bleiker, Sara E. Davies, and Richard Devetak.
New York: Routledge, 2008, p. 138.

Failed States as Safe Havens

To combat this enemy, the US government decided to increase its Special Operations Forces by 15 per cent and its [US Army Civil Affairs & Psychological Operations Command] by 33 per cent. It also stated that US forces would have to maintain a long-term, low-visibility presence in many areas of the world where the US does not traditionally operate. Of particular concern was the potential for so-called 'failed states' to act as safe havens for this new type of enemy. This had been a central theme of US foreign policy since 9/11. For example, in its 2002 National Security Strategy, the US government stated it was 'now threatened less by conquering states than . . . by failing ones'.

Beyond the obvious concern with Afghanistan, much of the focus fell upon Africa in general and its horn in particular. As a result, the US National Security Strategy published in March 2006 acknowledged that 'our security depends upon partnering with Africans to strengthen fragile and failing states and bring ungoverned areas under the control of effective democracies'. The problem with this approach is that there is not always a strong correlation between state failure and the proliferation of terrorist organizations, or indeed transnational security challenges more generally.

> *Even terrorists, it would seem, require a degree of political order to conduct their activities.*

Arguably the archetypal case in point is Somalia: collapsed state par excellence and the focus of much US counterterrorism activity since 9/11. However, Somalia has not become a major safe haven for terrorist organizations in spite of the ascendance of political Islam and the lack of effective government institutions. For one thing, until the middle of 2006, Islamic extremists struggled to gain ascendancy over more moderate Islamic voices within Somalia. For example, in 2005,

US intelligence gathering in Somalia produced no evidence of al-Qa'ida bases or that Al Itihad Al Islamiya [a militant Islamic group in Somalia], was operating as one of its subsidiaries.

Lawlessness Hurts Terrorists

As Ken Menkhaus has persuasively argued, there are six main reasons that explain this state of affairs. First, terrorist cells and bases are much more exposed to international counter-terrorist action in zones of state collapse where US Special Forces could violate state sovereignty regularly and with impunity. The US air strikes in January 2007 against al-Qa'ida suspects in Somalia are a case in point. Second, areas of state collapse tend to be inhospitable and dangerous, particularly for foreigners. Consequently, since few foreigners choose to reside in such environments, foreign terror cells will find it very difficult to blend into the local population and retain the degree of secrecy necessary to conduct their activities. A third factor is the double-edged nature of the lawlessness that accompanies situations of state collapse: While lawlessness reduces the risk of apprehension by law enforcement agencies, it increases the likelihood that terror cells will suffer from more common crimes such as kidnapping, extortion or assassination. As Menkhaus suggests, 'it appears that lawlessness can inhibit rather than facilitate certain types of lawless behavior'. A fourth problem is that any terrorists would be susceptible to betrayal by Somalis looking to ingratiate themselves with the US authorities. Fifth, Somalia represents an environment in which it is very difficult to stay neutral and outside the inter-clan rivalries. Relatively mundane activities such as hiring personnel or renting buildings will inevitably be seen as evidence of taking sides and once this perception has been established the external actor in question becomes a legitimate target of reprisals by rival clans. Finally the collapse of the Somali state has left it without the usual array of 'soft' Western targets such as embassies and businesses. As a result, Somalia is more likely to be used as a transit point for materiel than to act as a more permanent base for cells. Even terrorists, it would seem, require a degree of political order to conduct their activities. The 'security paradox' identified by Menkhaus is that at least in the short term, attempts to resurrect effective state institutions in Somalia may create an environment that is more, not less, conducive to terrorist cells basing themselves in the country. It would appear that terrorist organizations prefer to operate out of weak states with corruptible personnel such as Kenya, Indonesia, Pakistan, the Philippines, and Yemen rather than collapsed states. The front lines of the long war [against terrorism] should be redrawn accordingly.

Worldwide, the Islamic Religion Is the Cause of Terrorism

Daniel Greenfield

Daniel Greenfield is a New York–based writer and commentator. In the following viewpoint, written for a Canadian newspaper, he argues that the Koran and Islam advocate violence against non-Muslims. As a result, Greenfield says, Islamic political actors can always increase their credibility by attacks on non-Muslims. He argues that most terrorist attacks have nothing to do with the victims but are instead an expression of internal conflict within Islamic states, with both sides killing bystanders to increase their own popularity. Greenfield concludes that Islam itself—not poverty, political alienation, or historical injustice—is the cause of terrorism.

As you read, consider the following questions:

1. To what does Greenfield trace what he calls the two-sided concept of terrorism?

2. Why does Greenfield say there are very few moderate Muslims?

3. According to Greenfield, what is the ideological cause that encourages Islamic terrorism?

In the conventional political narrative the root causes of Islamic terrorism usually run the class warfare gamut from the generic oppression to outrage at Western foreign policy or more esoteric issues of globalism. And naturally like most people who look into a mirror to find the cause of someone else's anger, their reflection only repeats back to their own agenda.

Terrorism in the Islamic World

Surprisingly enough the root cause of Islamic terrorism has very little to do with any of these things, though they are moderately handy talking points when it comes to recruiting future terrorists or touching base with idiot leftist reporters. To understand the root cause requires understanding the function which terrorism serves in the Arab-Muslim world.

While Western liberals insist on viewing terrorism as a form of political or social activism, within the Muslim world terrorism is a two-sided tool, a way to create friction with an enemy without going to war while promoting the political standing of its leaders and backers. This two-sided concept of terrorism goes back to the nomadic days of bandit raiders that would carry out hit-and-run attacks that would bring in loot while raising the status of the tribal sheikh and the head of the raiding parties. Given enough time probing the enemy's weakness and raising the stature of the sheikh such attacks might escalate into all-out wars. And while such tactics may seem primitive, Mohammed [the founder of Islam] was able to leverage them to turn his newly created Islamic cult into a major player in the region.

In modern times, the driving ideological force behind Arab-Muslim terrorism has been to recreate a single great state to replace the splintered colonial entities left behind by the destruction of the Ottoman Empire [an Islamic Turkish empire that broke apart in 1923]. It was an ancient tribal goal, and one that Mohammed's followers had come closest to achieving in the Arab version of the Thousand Year Reich [Hitler's vision of a Nazi empire]. Modern versions of this might vary from the Islamic Caliphate [a vision of a religious Islamic empire] to the secular Arab Nationalist version that would be a socialist dictatorship run by someone like [Egypt's Gamal Abdel] Nasser or Saddam [Hussein of Iraq]. So while the ideology might vary, the underlying idea was always the same. One great state under one great ruler, who would demonstrate his fitness to rule by subjugating the enemy and thereby bring all of the region under his rule.

Under the ancient raiding codes, showing the most boldness and inflicting the most damage by striking at the enemy demonstrates that fitness to rule. This form of Arab-Muslim internal rivalry routinely spills over into external wars and terrorism, as both sides seek to prove their superiority by killing as many infidels as possible.

In practice no Islamic virtue is greater than that of defeating infidels and heretics. That single-minded approach allowed Islam to expand from an obscure cult to an empire.

Terrorism Is About Internal Conflicts

So [al Qaeda terrorist leader] Osama bin Laden's tribal religious conflict with the Saudi rulers was fought with the Soviets and then with America and Europe, more than with the House of Saud [the rulers of Saudi Arabia] itself. Using the pretext of the US troops that the House of Saud had brought in to protect themselves from Saddam [who invaded neighboring Kuwait in 1990], bin Laden was able to gain religious imprimatur for a war on America to build status for his claim to rule over the holiest place in Islam. The Saudis in turn had been funding a covert war on America for the same reason, as well as to divert wannabe bin Ladens from trying to seize power.

In the same way Hamas and Fatah [both militant Palestinian factions] addressed their rivalry for nearly two decades by competing to see who could kill more Israelis. Hamas's greater viciousness and murderousness won it the support of Palestinian Arabs, allowing them to triumph in elections and seize Gaza. While Western liberal observers have struggled to frame the conflict in terms of Hamas's social services or Fatah's corruption, these were only side issues. The main event was to demonstrate who could inflict more harm on the enemy. An indirect conflict [between] the Arab Nationalist Fatah and the Islamist Hamas for power over the Palestinian Authority cost the lives of numerous Israelis and foreign tourists, and it had next to nothing to do with any of the usual propaganda complaints about checkpoints or the wall of separation or even the desire for a Palestinian state, which the terrorism repeatedly sidelined. It had to do with an internal conflict expressed indirectly, a problem that is the root cause of much of Islamic terrorism.

It really does not matter what Israel does, or what America does, or what England and France or Denmark do.

That problem is also why there are fairly few actual moderate Muslims. When showing strength or inflicting harm against the enemy is key to leadership, moderation is an express train to nowhere. As terrorists have repeatedly demonstrated, every single Islamic religious law and practice can be set aside in the interest of killing infidels. That is because in practice no Islamic virtue is greater than that of defeating infidels and heretics. That single-minded approach allowed Islam to expand from an obscure cult to an empire. If Judaism embraces study and Christianity embraces evangelism as their key attributes, Islam embraces conquest. There would be no Islam without conquest. There can be no Islamic expansion today without it.

Within this framework, terrorism allows different groups to jockey for power by demonstrating that their way is best, when it comes to that fundamental virtue of killing infidels and forcing them to submit to their authority. All the while avoiding an open and outright war, which they are certain to lose. Terrorism allows Arab and Muslim nations to carry on covert wars and allows for the rise of local chiefs who conduct those wars, from the late and unlamented Yasir Arafat [a former Palestinian leader] to Osama bin Laden, [Lebanese terrorist group Hezbollah leader Hasan] Nasrallah or [Iraqi Islamic leader] Muqata al Sadr. Virtually every part of the world today has such chiefs or wannabe chiefs whose followers carry out bombings and murders in their name.

Propaganda and Reality

While the local pretexts may vary, Western observers err by confusing the propaganda with reality. Hitler did not invade Poland for any of the reasons he claimed he did, no more than Japan invaded China [in 1937] to protect the region from Europe. Like the mythical raped Belgian nuns of [World War I], propaganda is not motive, and it is startling to note the great eagerness with which supposed regional analysts treat propaganda as motive, rather than pretext at best.

It really does not matter what Israel does, or what America does, or what England and France or Denmark do. Being provocative or not only affects short-term reactions, not the long-term reality of the ideological causes of the conflict itself. And that ideological cause remains the dream of a great Islamic state with limitless boundaries, bringing all of the world into the Dar al Islam [places where Islam can be practiced safely.] That is the great dream for which Mohammed's warriors rode out with blood-red swords, and in succeeding centuries rampaged across the Middle East, Asia and even Europe. It is the post-Ottoman dream as well, and it is behind the diverse Islamic terrorist and guerrilla uprisings across the world today.

But that dream requires leadership, and that struggle for leadership has also indirectly led to much of the terrorism in the 20th century and the 21st, as Arab leaders and Islamic militias have all struggled to define the cause around individuals. Osama bin Laden's videos, like Arafat's infamous speech at the UN [in 1974, in which he said, "I have come bearing an olive branch and a freedom fighter's gun"], are part of that larger narrative, a story of "personal greatness" weighed by the value of the only coin acceptable in the Middle East and demonstrated through the corpses of innocent men and women who belong to the "tribes of the enemy".

In Latin America, Islam Is Not Linked to Terrorism

Vitória Peres de Oliveira

Vitória Peres de Oliveira is an associate professor of religion at the Universidade Federal de Juiz de Fora in Minas Gerais, Brazil. In the following viewpoint, she argues that in Latin America, Muslim communities are integrated into the population and are often relatively well-off. She also states that Muslim communities are small, often include native converts, and have relatively little interest in international Islamic political grievances. She concludes that Muslim communities in Latin America are not linked to terrorism.

As you read, consider the following questions:

1. According to de Oliveira, in which Latin American countries is the Muslim population more than 1 percent of the total population?
2. What examples does de Oliveira give of the transnational character of Islam?
3. What is Wahhabi Islam, according to de Oliveira?

The number of Muslims in Latin America, according to Muslim sources, is about 6 million, or 1.2 percent of the population of almost 500 million. According to other sources,

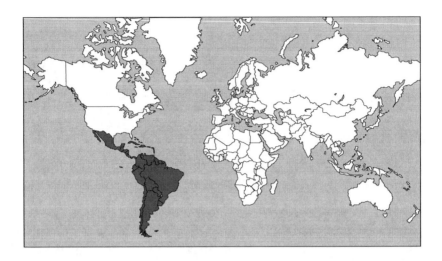

it's much lower. In most Latin American countries the Muslim population is less than 1 percent of the total, except in Argentina, Trinidad, Tobago, Guyana and Suriname. Most of these numbers are estimates given by Muslim sources and may have been inflated. In Brazil there is a wide discrepancy between the Muslim estimate—1 million to 1.5 million and the official census figure, 27,239; and also among the Muslim sources themselves. Some say half a million, some say 1 million, some say 1.5 million.

Low Numbers of Muslims

Of that total, there are many Muslims in name only. Not all are practicing or worshipping in the mosque. In Brazil, at most of the mosques visited, there is a discrepancy of one-third or greater between the number of the faithful present and the number of the faithful that the mosque says it has. This also seems to be the case in other countries. The Muslim population is mostly Sunni, basically in line with the proportion worldwide, which is about 84 percent Sunni and 16 percent Shi'ite. [Sunni and Shi'ite, or Shia, are the two major Muslim denominations.]

We can talk about two models of communities in Latin America. First, communities founded by immigrants. We have immigrants from India, Pakistan or Indonesia who came to Suriname, Guyana, and Trinidad and Tobago. The proportion of Muslims in these countries in relation to the population is the largest in Latin America, but in absolute terms, their number is low. Both Guyana and Suriname are members of the Organization of Islamic Countries, so the population numbers in those countries are more reliable.

The second model is Muslim communities founded by immigrants. Syrian, Lebanese and Palestinian immigrants arrived at the end of the 19th and first half of the 20th centuries. This is the case for most countries of South America. These communities followed similar stages, and because of their economic success ran the risk of being diluted into the society at large. That's why the aim of the first organizations founded in the 1920s was to bring the communities together around the native linguistic and religious traditions. Thus, their religion acquired an ethnic character. The communities were started as closed groups and were not open to diffusion outside of the original group. This ethnic character began to lose strength from the end of the 1990s when Islam entered the international scene in a big way, and individuals began to show interest in conversion.

The Arab immigrants who started these communities now belong to an economic, social and cultural position that is well above average in the societies of which they are part.

Then we have other kinds of communities—Muslim communities founded by new Muslims or converts, which is a quite recent phenomenon. We have a few examples of those communities in Mexico, Haiti, Cuba and Ecuador. These new Muslims are generally students who converted to Islam while studying in Europe and the United States; some then go to Muslim countries to learn more about Islam and diffusion. These communities are much more active and dynamic than those started by immigrants. Muslim sources suggest that converts account for approximately 1 percent of all Muslims throughout Latin America.

The case of Mexico is interesting because, despite some sources stating that 10 percent of the Syrians and Lebanese who immigrated there were Muslims, the Muslim community was only started in 1994 by a new Muslim who converted to Islam while he was studying in Florida. He then studied in Saudi Arabia for two years, went back to Mexico and is working hard to spread Islam in Mexico. There is also a unique situation. . . . That's 300 native Mayan Indians from the Chiapas region [in Mexico] were converted by a small group of Spanish Muslims, who went there to spread the word of Islam.

Characteristics of Islam in Latin America

So now I will present some facts that can help us understand the presence of Islam in Latin America.

First, the Arab immigrants who started these communities now belong to an economic, social and cultural position that is well above average in the societies of which they are part. Unlike European Muslims, these societies are not associated with social exclusion. This factor must be taken into account: The position and easy absorption of Muslims immigrating into Latin American cultures is an important factor to consider when examining Muslim communities in Latin America.

Number two: New Muslims or converts are playing a growing role. Currently, they represent the only possibility for Islamic growth in Latin America, because the immigration of Muslims has been declining. New Muslims and converts place greater emphasis on the religious and puritanical aspects of their practice and make greater efforts to attract new participants. Their presence in the communities founded by immigrants produces some tension between them and people who were born Muslim, with the converts complaining that the older members are not very open to them, and that there is little dynamism with regard to the spread of religion. In Brazil, new Muslims are starting to engage in activities designed to spread Islam to Brazil. The presence of converts has led to greater emphasis on the demand for religious rights for the Muslim community in the public sphere and a lessening of interest in international political questions related to the Middle East.

Number three: It is important to consider the transnational character of this religion and the constant movement of its members through Muslim countries. Sheikhs come to run religious activities; born and new Muslims go to study and to the pilgrimage to Mecca [an Islamic holy city in Saudi Arabia]. In Brazil now we have two Brazilian-born Muslims who studied in Saudi Arabia and became sheikhs, who speak Portuguese in our Brazilian culture, and are now leading Muslim activities in our country. There are new Muslims also studying [in] Islamic countries such as Saudi Arabia and Sudan, including one ex-evangelist minister, who is in Syria. This transnationality is not a characteristic of Islam but rather of religion in our times, and is an ingredient that makes the discerning of possible trends seem more complex.

Each community or mosque is independent of the rest and therefore has its own characteristics, more resembling Protestants than Roman Catholics.

Number four: The role of international help by Muslim countries in the Latin American community is another significant feature of Islam in Latin America. It is a duty of a Muslim country to support the practice of religion of Muslims abroad. Let's not forget that other religions do that too. Most of this financial assistance comes from the Saudi government and international organizations. According to Latin American Muslim Unity (LAMU), the governments of Saudi Arabia, Qatar and Kuwait have invested about $20 million in the expansion of Islam in Latin America. . . .

Saudi Arabia follows what's called Wahhabi Islam. This is a rigid and puritanical version of Islam. Wahhabism is not a Muslim sect, such as the Shi'ite sect, for example, but is a reform movement within Sunni Islam. Reform movements are aimed at refining the religion and to returning to the origins that are common to all religions. Wahhabism, however, has been used as an influence by radical and extremist Muslim sectors. This does not mean that the Saudi Wahhabi movement is necessarily connected to radical groups. The Wahhabi influence has led to Latin American Islam becoming more rigid and puritanical in its religious practice, but it has not been related to political activities. In the Brazilian mosques studied, Wahhabism is one influence, but is not the only one.

It is important not to demonize those Latin American Muslim communities. This will not be good for anyone.

Number five: Related to the problem of influence is the role the Internet has played for new Muslims. Visiting different sites is common and thus they have contact with varied tendencies within Islam.

Number six: Each community or mosque is independent of the rest and therefore has its own characteristics, more resembling Protestants than Roman Catholics. The sheikh, mainly in a Sunni community, is a religious leader but is not seen by the participants as someone who they necessarily have to obey. The fact that the communities are outside of Muslim countries also leaves the members free to follow or not follow precepts preached.

Margarita Island

Some observations about the triple frontier in Margarita Island [a tourist destination on the border between Argentina, Brazil, and Paraguay with a large Muslim population]: There are Muslim communities in two cities, Foz [do] Iguaçu in Brazil and Ciudad del Este in Paraguay. There is no community in Puerto Iguazú, Argentina. Between the first two cities there is a daily circulation of the population with only a bridge separating them. There are various other ethnic groups. A particular characteristic of this community is that the number of Shi'ites represents almost half of all Muslims in Foz [do] Iguaçu, which is not typical of communities elsewhere in Brazil and in Latin America. The sheikhs who live the local religious practice only speak Arabic. The communities have no new Muslims or converts yet. At the end of 1999 and after September 11th [2001, when terrorists attacked the United States] many people left the region, and the population has fallen by about one-third. According to a Muslim source, in spite of having a population of 4,000 Muslims in Foz [do] Iguaçu, only about one hundred frequent the mosque there regularly.

Margarita Island has a population of about 4,000 Muslims, mostly Lebanese and Palestinian, mainly merchants. It can be said, then, that both the communities have a more ethnic character and their immigration is more recent. In this type of community it's quite common for people to stay in contact with their home countries and show interest in their political issues. As for setting up terrorist cells, this has never been proven. An Argentine researcher who started investigating the area told me she had the impression the media had exaggerated the threat in relation to the Muslim communities of the region and that the reality is quite different than that portrayed. The communities are no different than the other ones studied. A large illicit economy thrives in the area, but this does not necessarily mean that the Muslim community as a whole is involved.

Personally, I believe that what should be fought is the terror and the criminals. They are not Muslims, Buddhists or Christians; they are criminals and terrorists. The communities are integrated or are in that process, and in general, they love the countries to where they have moved. It is important to get to know them and not to associate Islam with terror there. It is important not to demonize those Latin American Muslim communities. This will not be good for anyone. Islam is a religion like any other, and [Muslim] communities are a concrete manifestation of the religion experienced by individual human beings. Recently, in Rio de Janeiro the Muslim community expelled two members because they started a site called Islamic Jihad where they espoused radical and nationalistic ideals. The community said they did not want to have anything to do with them.

In closing, for Islam to grow in Latin America, it will need Latin American converts because the migratory movement of Muslims has declined. In my opinion, the presence of the converts is already bringing strong changes to the original communities. I can't say whether Islam will grow in Latin America, but what can be said is that [Muslim] numbers are very, very small and their visibility is more because of the international media than because of their actual presence. Let's try and understand this religion in Latin America and its followers without any fear or prejudice.

Periodical and Internet Sources Bibliography

The following articles have been selected to supplement the diverse views presented in this chapter.

Eddy Acevedo   "Threat of Terrorism in Latin America," TheAmericano.com, January 7, 2010. http://theamericano.com.

Ethan Bueno de Mesquita   "Does Poverty Lead to Violence? (The Other View)," *Chris Blattman* (blog), April 4, 2011. http://chrisblattman.com.

Andrew Cline   "Poverty Does Not Cause Terrorism," *American Spectator*, January 7, 2010.

Douglas Farah   "The Growing Terrorism Challenges from Latin America," International Assessment and Strategy Center, February 18, 2007. www.strategycenter.net.

Daniel Meierrieks and Tim Krieger   "What Causes Terrorism?," Social Science Research Network, June 8, 2009. http://papers.ssrn.com.

Robin Pomeroy   "U.S. Policy Post 9/11 Has Increased Terorrism: Syria," Reuters, September 11, 2008. www.reuters.com.

Christopher Preble   "Failed States Don't Cause Terrorism," RealClearWorld, June 27, 2011. www.realclearworld.com.

Philip Slater   "The Root Causes of Terrorism and Why No One Wants to End Them," *Huffington Post*, October 25, 2008. www.huffingtonpost.com.

Liana Sun Wyler   "Weak and Failing States: Evolving Security Threats and U.S. Policy," *CRS Report for Congress*, August 28, 2008.

GLOBALVIEWPOINTS

CHAPTER 2

Human Rights and the War on Terror

In Britain, Respect for Human Rights Helps in the War on Terror

Lord Phillips of Worth Matravers

Lord Phillips is president of the Supreme Court of the United Kingdom. In the following viewpoint, he explains that British courts adhere to the Human Rights Act and also must follow the laws of the European community. As a result, he says, British courts uphold the rights of terrorism suspects and must provide them with fair trials and protect them from torture. He argues that this adherence to human rights reduces resentment and supports democratic society. He concludes that human rights are a crucial weapon in the War on Terror.

As you read, consider the following questions:

1. According to Lord Phillips, what was the ruling by the Strasbourg court in *Chahal v. United Kingdom*?

2. What does Lord Phillips say were the provisions of the first Control Orders issued?

3. What does Lord Phillips believe that Home Secretary Charles Clarke failed to appreciate?

Lord Phillips, "The Gresham Special Lecture 2010: The Challenges of the Supreme Court," Gresham College, June 8, 2010. Copyright of the Supreme Court of the United Kingdom. All rights reserved. Reprinted by permission.

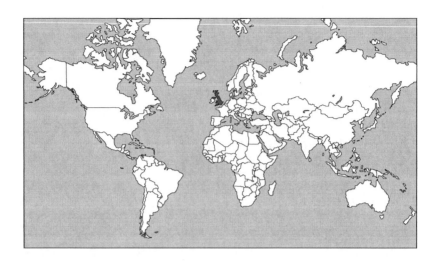

The power of judicial review is one that judges invented in order to make sure that state officials comply with what we call the 'rule of law'. 50 years ago judicial review cases were very rare, but now they are the most important part of the diet of the Supreme Court [of the United Kingdom].

Judicial Review

One thing that the courts were not allowed to review were Acts of Parliament, for no one could challenge the lawfulness of an Act of Parliament. That has now changed. . . . When we joined the EEC [European Economic Community], Parliament passed a statute that gave precedence to community law. So the Supreme Court can, and indeed must, refuse to give effect to an Act of Parliament that is contrary to EC [European Community] law. That does not happen very often.

More common are human rights challenges and these now constitute a major part of our diet. The European Convention on Human Rights [officially known as the Convention for the Protection of Human Rights and Fundamental Freedoms] is not an EC treaty. It is a treaty that binds the much wider membership of the Council of Europe [that includes all countries in Europe]. Inhabitants of any member state who consider that their human rights have been infringed can make a claim against their government before the European Court of Human Rights at Strasbourg [France]. Before the Human Rights Act was passed in 1998 those in this country could not base a claim in the courts of this country on infringement of their human rights. They had to go off to Strasbourg.

The Human Rights Act has changed all that. Citizens can now claim compensation from the government in the English courts if their human rights are infringed. And it is the duty of the courts to take account of the decisions of the Strasbourg court when we are dealing with human rights claims. The consequence of our doing so is that we sometimes have to rule that government action is unlawful, or even that parliamentary legislation is incompatible with the human rights convention. This has caused the government a considerable problem when trying to deal with terrorism.

'The real threat to the life of the nation, in the sense of a people living in accordance with its traditional laws and political values, comes not from terrorism but from laws such as these'.

Deportation

Let me explain the nature of the problem. In 1996, in a case called *Chahal v. United Kingdom*, the Strasbourg court ruled that it is contrary to the human rights convention for us to deport an illegal immigrant if he will be at risk of torture or inhuman treatment if he is sent home, however great a risk that he may pose to this country. But at the same time the Strasbourg court has ruled that you cannot lock up an illegal immigrant without a trial just because you have grounds to suspect that he is a terrorist. If you want to lock him up you have to prove that he is a terrorist.

There is an exception to this. The convention permits a country to derogate from the prohibition of detention without trial, but only 'to the extent strictly required by the exigencies of the situation "in time of war or other public emergency threatening the life of the nation"'. Those words are important.

After 9/11 [September 21, 2001, terrorist attacks on the United States] the British government decided that the threat of terrorism in Britain was such as to amount to a public emergency threatening the life of the nation and purported, on that ground, to derogate from the convention. It did so only in respect of 'foreign nationals present in the United Kingdom' who were suspected of being concerned in terrorism. Relying on this derogation, Parliament then passed the Anti-Terrorism, Crime and Security Act 2001. This permitted an alien to be detained indefinitely if the Home Secretary reasonably suspected that he was a terrorist and believed that he was a threat to national security but was unable to deport him because he would be at risk of inhuman treatment in his own country. The Home Secretary immediately exercised this power by locking up a number of aliens. He made it plain to them that if they wanted, voluntarily, to go back to their own countries, they would be free to do so. They did not. Instead they appealed to the court that their right to liberty under the human rights convention had been infringed.

They challenged their detention on two grounds. First they argued that there was not 'a public emergency threatening the life of the nation'. Secondly they argued that the derogation was unlawful because it went beyond what was 'strictly required by the exigencies of the situation'.

Their challenge to their detention went up to the House of Lords, which sat nine strong rather than the usual five to hear the case, and they were successful. The majority of the House of Lords held that there was a 'public emergency threatening the life of the nation' so that the derogation from the convention was permissible. Lord Hoffmann disagreed. He said:

'The real threat to the life of the nation, in the sense of a people living in accordance with its traditional laws and political values, comes not from terrorism but from laws such as these. That is the true measure of what terrorism may achieve.'

Where all the Law Lords agreed was in holding that the terms of the derogation and the provisions of the act were unlawful in that they went beyond what was 'strictly required by the exigencies of the situation'.

In so holding they dismissed a submission by the Attorney General on behalf of the government that it was not for the courts rather than the government to assess the proportionality of anti-terrorism measures. This is what Lord Bingham said:

'The function of independent judges charged to interpret and apply the law is universally recognised as a cardinal feature of the modern democratic state, a cornerstone of the rule of law itself'.

It was Parliament that had given the courts the task of protecting human rights and that was a *very specific, wholly democratic mandate*.

Human Rights vs. Terrorism

There were three reasons why the Law Lords held that this legislation went too far. The first was the importance that the United Kingdom has attached, since at least Magna Carta [an important English law document from 1215], to personal liberty. The second was that the measures applied only to aliens. There were plenty of terrorist suspects who were British subjects. How could it be necessary to lock up the foreign suspects without trial if it was not necessary to lock up the British suspects? Finally, the measures permitted those detained to opt to leave the country. If they were so dangerous how could it be appropriate to leave them free to continue their terrorist

activities overseas? So the House of Lords quashed the derogation order and declared that the relevant provisions of the act
were incompatible with the convention.

Parliament's reaction to this judgment was to rescind the
legislation and pass a new act—the Prevention of Terrorism
Act 2005. This among other things empowers the Secretary of
State to place restrictions on the movements and activities of
terrorist suspects by making them subject to control orders.
The restrictions must not, however, be so severe as to amount
to deprivation of liberty, or once again they will run foul of
the requirements of the human rights convention. It is not an
easy question to decide where you draw the line, and that
question is ultimately one for the courts, and it is one that has
been keeping the courts busy.

---

*The Secretary of State was often not prepared to disclose
his reasons for suspecting that a person was involved in
terrorism. . . . How could there be a fair trial in such circumstances?*

The first batch of control orders imposed by the Home
Secretary required the suspects to stay confined within small
apartments for 18 hours a day, and placed stringent restrictions on where they could go and whom they could see in the
remaining six hours. These orders were challenged and a divi-
sion of the Court of Appeal over which I presided ruled that
they were unlawful in that the restrictions that they imposed
amounted to deprivation of liberty.

The Home Secretary immediately imposed modified control orders in place of the old ones. These were not nearly as
restrictive and, in contrast to the old ones, were specially tai-
lored to meet the circumstances of the individual suspect.

The curfew periods were reduced to 14, or in some cases,
12 hours a day. These in their turn were challenged in the
courts, but were held not to amount to deprivation of liberty.

Subsequently the issue of when a control order amounts to deprivation of liberty was considered by the House of Lords, together with another issue that I am going to come to. The House upheld our decision that an 18-hour curfew amounted to deprivation of liberty. Lord Brown suggested that 16 hours was the maximum permissible curfew period. There was some, inconclusive, discussion as to the extent to which other restrictions, when added to a curfew period, could tip the scales when deciding whether there was a deprivation of liberty.

That question reared its head again in the latest control order case, in which the Supreme Court has yet to deliver judgment.

Control Orders and Transparency

Meanwhile the imposition of control orders had been attacked on another front. They can only be imposed where the Home Secretary has reasonable grounds for suspecting that the suspect has been involved in terrorism and that the control order is necessary to protect members of the public from terrorism. Article 6 of the human rights convention guarantees the right to a fair trial.

This means that the suspect must have a right to challenge the control order in the courts and the procedure adopted by the courts must be fair. This raised a problem. The Secretary of State was often not prepared to disclose his reasons for suspecting that a person was involved in terrorism, for to do so might prejudice ongoing security operations. How could there be a fair trial in such circumstances? The same problem sometimes arose in the case of immigrants whom the Home Security wished to deport on security grounds.

Parliament came up with an ingenious answer. It created a special court called SIAC [Special Immigration Appeals Commission]. SIAC sat in public to hear evidence that did not have security implications. Where, however, evidence could

Secret Evidence and the Detention of Foreign Terrorism Suspects in the United Kingdom

In *A v. UK [United Kingdom]*, the Grand Chamber [of the European Court of Human Rights] unanimously held that there had been a violation of the right . . . to have the lawfulness of detention decided by a court in the cases of four of those who were detained under Part IV of the Anti-Terrorism, Crime and Security Act 2001. The court held that the evidence on which the state relied to support the principal allegations made against the four individuals was largely to be found in the closed material and was therefore not disclosed to the individuals or their lawyers. It said that special advocates could not perform their function, of safeguarding the detainee's interests during closed hearings, in any useful way unless the detainee was provided with sufficient information about the allegations against him to enable him to give effective instructions to the special advocate. There was a violation of the right to a judicial determination of the legality of detention because the four detainees were not in a position effectively to challenge the allegations against them.

Joint Committee on Human Rights,
Enhancing Parliament's Role in
Relation to Human Rights Judgments,
House of Lords/House of Commons,
March 9, 2010, p. 16.

not be made public, SIAC would sit in private to hear it, and the suspect himself would not be allowed to be present. Instead he would be represented by a Special Advocate, who had security clearance. The Special Advocate would argue the suspect's case in relation to the secret evidence, but he would not be allowed to communicate that evidence to his client.

Suspects challenged this procedure on the ground that they could not have a fair trial if they were not allowed to know the details of the case against them. The government argued that the suspect's right to a fair trial would be satisfactorily protected by the Special Advocate procedure. The case went up to the House of Lords. It is the one to which I have already referred when discussing the length of control orders. Each member of the House gave his or her own opinion. These raised great problems for the lower courts, because they were unable to agree on precisely what the Law Lords had decided. They agreed that in most cases it would be possible, in one way or another, to give the suspect a fair trial.

But what if the security services were not prepared to disclose to the suspect the essence, or gist, of the case against him, so that he was left completely in the dark as to why he had been made subject to a control order. At least one member of the House, Lord Brown, suggested that if the case against the suspect was so strong that no challenge could conceivably succeed, then there was no need to tell him even the gist of the case against him. It was not clear, however, whether Lord Brown was out on a limb on this, or whether the other Law Lords agreed with him.

So, you can guess what happened. Three more control order cases came up to the House of Lords.

We ruled that if the Secretary of State was not prepared to tell those subject to the control orders the essence of the case against them, he had to lift the control orders.

The suspects subject to the control orders complained that they had been told nothing of the cases against them and that their human rights had been infringed because they had not had a fair trial. The government relied on the speech of Lord

Brown in the previous case and argued that if there were overwhelming grounds for believing that the suspects were involved in terrorism, it was not unfair to impose the control orders, even if the suspects could not be told the case against them.

I was presiding on this appeal. Before we could hear it the Grand Chamber of the Strasbourg court gave a judgment which dealt quite categorically with the point. They said that where the Secretary of State's decision was based solely or decisively on material the gist of which was not disclosed to the suspect, the suspect did not have a fair trial.

We felt that we had no option but to follow this decision of the Strasbourg court, although it is fair to say that the majority of us thought that the Strasbourg court was right.

So we ruled that if the Secretary of State was not prepared to tell those subject to the control orders the essence of the case against them, he had to lift the control orders. In a number of cases he has chosen to do just that.

Upholding the Rule of Law

I have been describing to you a number of cases in which the action taken by government to deal with terrorist suspects has been held to be unlawful by the House of Lords or the Supreme Court. They are only examples. They have led some sections of the media to attack the Human Rights Act, or even the judges who have to apply it. Charles Clarke, when Home Secretary, when giving evidence to a parliamentary committee protested:

> 'The judiciary bears not the slightest responsibility for protecting the public and sometimes seem utterly unaware of the implications of their decisions for our society.'

Charles Clarke failed to appreciate that it is the duty of the judiciary to apply the laws that have been enacted by Parliament. It was Parliament that decreed that judges should apply the human rights convention and, when doing so, to take account of the judgments of the Strasbourg court.

Having said that I should add that, in my opinion, the enactment of the Human Rights Act by the previous administration was an outstanding contribution to the upholding of the rule of law in this country and one for which it deserves great credit. Because it requires the courts to scrutinise not merely executive action but Acts of Parliament to make sure that these respect human rights, the act has given the Supreme Court some of the functions of a constitutional court. Drawing the right line between protecting the rights of the individual and respecting the supremacy of Parliament is, I believe, our greatest challenge.

I would like to end by reading a passage from the speech of Lord Hope in a case which was concerned with whether it was safe to send terrorist suspects home to their own countries.

Most people in Britain, I suspect, would be astonished at the amount of care, time and trouble that has been devoted to the question whether it will be safe for the aliens to be returned to their own countries.

> In each case the Secretary of State has issued a certificate under section 33 of the Anti-Terrorism, Crime and Immigration Act 2001 that the aliens' removal from the United Kingdom would be conducive to the public good. The measured language of the statute scarcely matches the harm that they would wish to inflict upon our way of life, if they were at liberty to do so. Why hesitate, people may ask. Surely the sooner they are got rid of the better. On their own heads be it if their extremist views expose them to the risk of ill-treatment when they get home.

That however is not the way the rule of law works. The lesson of history is that depriving people of its protection because of their beliefs or behaviour, however obnoxious, leads to the disintegration of society. A democracy cannot survive in such an atmosphere, as events in Europe in the 1930s [with the rise of fascism] so powerfully demonstrated. It was to eradicate this evil that the European Convention on Human Rights, following the example of the Universal Declaration of Human Rights by the General Assembly of the United Nations on 10 December 1948, was prepared for the governments of European countries to enter into.

The so-called 'war against terrorism' is not so much a military as an ideological battle. Respect for human rights is a key weapon in this ideological battle.

The most important word in this document appears in article 1, and it is repeated time and time again in the following articles. It is the word 'everyone'. The rights and fundamental freedoms that the convention guarantees are not just for some people. They are for everyone. No one, however dangerous, however disgusting, however despicable, is excluded. Those who have no respect for the rule of law—even those who would seek to destroy it—are in the same position as everyone else.

The paradox that this system produces is that, from time to time, much time and effort has to be given to the protection of those who may seem to be the least deserving. Indeed it is just because their cases are so unattractive that the law must be especially vigilant to ensure that the standards to which everyone is entitled are adhered to. The rights that the aliens invoke in this case were designed to enshrine values that are essential components of any modern democratic society: the right not to be tortured or subjected to inhuman or degrading treatment, the right to liberty and the right to a fair trial. There is no room for discrimination here. Their protection must be given to everyone.

It would be so easy, if it were otherwise, for minority groups of all kinds to be persecuted by the majority. We must not allow this to happen. Feelings of the kind that the aliens' beliefs and conduct give rise to must be resisted for however long it takes to ensure that they have this protection.

Human Rights as a Weapon

To this I would add this comment. The so-called 'war against terrorism' is not so much a military as an ideological battle. Respect for human rights is a key weapon in that ideological battle. Since the Second World War we in Britain have welcomed to the United Kingdom millions of immigrants from all corners of the globe, many of them refugees from countries where human rights were not respected. It is essential that they and their children and grandchildren should be confident that their adopted country treats them without discrimination and with due respect for their human rights.

If they feel that they are not being fairly treated, their consequent resentment will inevitably result in the growth of those who, actively or passively, are prepared to support terrorists who are bent on destroying our society. The Human Rights Act is not merely their safeguard. It is a vital part of the foundation of our fight against terrorism.

Europe's Misguided Focus on Human Rights Has Hampered the US War on Terror

Sally McNamara

Sally McNamara is a senior policy analyst in European affairs at the Heritage Foundation. In the following viewpoint, she argues that the European Union's focus on human rights and its condemnation of the United States has hurt US efforts to fight the War on Terror. She points especially to the European Union's efforts to restrict data sharing, its refusal to condemn the Lebanese militant Islamic group Hezbollah as a terrorist organization, and its criticism of US policies dealing with the detention and transport of terrorist suspects to other nations.

As you read, consider the following questions:

1. Where are many of America's strongest allies in the War on Terror, according to McNamara, and which does she single out in particular?

2. What programs that the EU has advanced in the name of counterterrorism does McNamara say are unnecessary?

3. With what counterterrorism success does McNamara credit CIA sites in Europe?

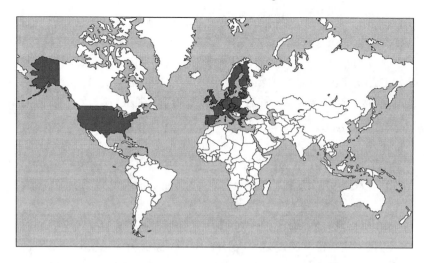

America needs allies to win the war on terrorism. Many of America's strongest allies in the fight against transnational terrorism are in Europe—most notably the United Kingdom. In addition to individual nation-states, the EU [the European Union] is also a partner of significance to the United States for purposes of counterterrorism.

Confrontation with the EU

Since the 9/11 [September 11, 2001] terrorist attacks [on the United States], the EU has become a major counterterrorist actor. Some EU policies have had a positive impact on the global war on terrorism—especially the production of a list of persons, groups, and entities whose financial assets will be frozen and to whom financial services are denied. However, many EU policies have obstructed U.S. counterterror efforts. For example, Brussels [the capital of the European Union] has long opposed U.S. renditions policy [where suspects are sent to some countries where they may be tortured] and has even threatened to sanction member states for hosting CIA [U.S. Central Intelligence Agency] sites in Europe. The EU also refuses to designate Hezbollah [a militant Lebanese Islamic group] as a Foreign Terrorist Organization, which would deny the terrorist entity a primary fund-raising base. And the European Parliament has legally stalled two vital data-transfer deals—the SWIFT [Society for Worldwide Interbank Financial Telecommunication] data-sharing agreement and the EU-U.S. Passenger Name Record (PNR) agreement.

Overall, the EU-U.S. counterterrorism relationship has been marked as much by confrontation as it has by cooperation. The U.S. must therefore continue to invest in its bilateral relationships with individual EU states, as well as formulating a new agenda for cooperation with the EU.

Before 9/11, just six of the EU's then 15 member states recognized terrorism as a special offense. In the aftermath of 9/11, EU member states began coordinating their national counterterrorism laws with one another and agreed to a common definition of terrorism. This common definition of terrorism effectively denied terrorists the sanctuary of border hopping to another member state where terrorism was not previously regarded as a specific offense. Crucially, the European Council also produced a list of persons, groups, and entities whose financial assets would be frozen and to whom financial services would henceforth be denied. This has proved to be one of the EU's most valuable contributions to counterterrorism to date since it has denied terrorists the freedom to operate and raise funds in Europe.

In 2004 and 2005, Europe was confronted with two major terrorist attacks on its soil. In March 2004, an al Qaeda–affiliated group remotely detonated 10 bombs on four Madrid commuter trains at the height of rush hour, killing 191 people and injuring more than 1,800. In July 2005, "homegrown" al Qaeda operatives acted as suicide bombers on multiple London public transportation targets, killing 52 people.

In light of these attacks, the EU implemented a number of additional counterterror measures. In 2004, EU leaders appointed a counterterrorism coordinator to audit members' implementation of EU policies. In 2005, the EU adopted a

British-inspired comprehensive counterterror strategy, outlining four strategic "strands of work" to prevent, protect, pursue, and respond to terrorism. And in 2008, the EU formally expanded its common definition of terrorism to criminalize three specific new offenses which had become necessary in light of the 3/11 [referring to bombings in Madrid, Spain, on March 11, 2004] and 7/7 [referring to bombings in London on July 7, 2005] attacks: (1) public provocation to commit a terrorist offense, (2) recruitment for terrorism, and (3) training for terrorism.

The EU has also advanced several unnecessary programs under the guise of countering terrorism. The EU has given greater authority to, and has gradually expanded the mandates of, ineffective institutions such as the European Police Office (Europol), Eurojust, and SitCen [Joint Situation Centre]. The EU's flagship European Arrest Warrant (EAW) program—whereby EU member states are obliged to render citizens to another member state upon request, without *prima facie* [at first appearance] evidence—was justified as a key counterterror measure. However, it has been used to extradite people for overwhelmingly far less serious offenses than transnational terrorism, including leaving a gas station without paying.

Complying with these measures diverts the antiterrorism resources of EU member states away from what they should really be doing and merely seeks to advance the EU's integrationist agenda.

Crippling human rights legislation has also been pursued in pursuit of "tolerance."

A Radical Legislative Agenda

The 7/7 attacks revealed that Europe is now facing "home-grown" terrorist attacks as well as those directed from abroad. Research carried out by the Heritage Foundation (June 2008) and the U.K.-based Change Institute (February 2008) demonstrated that foreign-born hate preachers and extremist clerics such as Abu Hamza [al-Masri], Tolga Dürbin, and Omar Bakri Mohammad have acted as primary recruiters of homegrown terrorists and inciters to terrorist acts. They have been responsible for sending European recruits to terrorist training camps—particularly in Afghanistan and Pakistan—for the purposes of further radicalization and logistical training.

This phenomenon is best addressed in two ways: (1) the exclusion of foreign-born hate preachers and extremist clerics and (2) the eradication of terrorist training camps. The EU has chosen instead, however, to focus its activism on two other issues: (1) combating the beliefs, ideologies, and narratives that underpin violent radicalization and (2) combating "Islamophobia." In November 2008, the EU's "Strategy for Combating Radicalisation and Recruitment to Terrorism" was published, which recommended identifying and encouraging moderate foreign imams to present a counter-radical case. However, this has already been tried—and has failed—in several EU member states. The previous U.K. Labour government courted foreign imams such as Sheikh Yusuf al-Qaradawi on the basis that al-Qaradawi is "a highly respected Islamic scholar." The former government has since had cause to regret that decision after discovering that al-Qaradawi has defended suicide bombings, called for the execution of homosexuals, and advised European Muslims to create "Muslim ghettos where they can avoid cultural assimilation and introduce sharia [Islamic] law."

Member states should also be wary of attempts to legislate against "Islamophobia," which was recommended by the Change Institute. Europe has behind it a catalog of failed public policies when it comes to promoting "equality." German Chancellor Angela Merkel is just one European leader who has come to the conclusion that multiculturalism has failed. Crippling human rights legislation has also been pursued in pursuit of "tolerance," including the EU's Charter of Fundamental Rights and the Council of Europe's European Convention on Human Rights (ECHR) [officially known as the Convention for the Protection of Human Rights and Fundamental Freedoms]. These policies have weakened, not strengthened, members' counterterrorism efforts. For example, British judges refused to make full use of control orders [that placed restrictions on suspected terrorists] mandated under the U.K.'s 2000 Terrorism Act on the grounds that 18-hour curfews may breach the convention's Article V clause on the right to liberty.

The U.S. should be wary of the EU's radical political agenda and of the way it spends money inside the United States for the purposes of furthering its favored political causes. This includes the funding of nonprofits and advocacy organizations to advance such controversial issues as:

- U.S. membership on the International Criminal Court,

- America's abolition of the death penalty,

- The standardization of international legal norms,

- The closing of the U.S. Guantánamo [Bay] detention facility, and

- Debating U.S. detention and rendition policies.

The EU-U.S. Counterterrorism Relationship

Despite an unprecedented display of transatlantic solidarity following the 9/11 terrorist attacks, the EU-U.S. counterterrorism relationship has been marked as much by confrontation as by cooperation. The Lisbon Treaty, which was introduced in 2009, has also seen a huge boost in powers for the European Parliament, which has flexed its legislative muscle to frustrate key U.S. counterterror policies.

Passenger Name Record (PNR) Agreement. The U.S. Air Transportation Safety Act of 2002 requires that the PNR data

"Of course we Europeans have an anti terror plan, Mr. President!," cartoon by Karlen Schley, www.CartoonStock.com. Copyright © Karlen Schley. Reproduction rights obtainable from www.CartoonStock.com.

of travelers to the U.S. are provided to American authorities before the arrival of planes in the U.S. In May 2004, the EU and the U.S. agreed that airlines operating U.S.-bound flights would provide the U.S. authorities with travelers' data contained in their reservation systems before the flight's departure. Being able to analyze the personal and financial data of passengers prior to departure, in conjunction with U.S. and international intelligence databases, allows analysts a further opportunity to spot any red flags and ultimately screen out potential terrorists.

However, the European Parliament argued that the 2004 agreement violated EU citizens' privacy rights. The European Parliament's objections revolved around the amount of PNR data transferred to the U.S. authorities, the length of time such data could be kept, the degree of redress available to European citizens in cases of data misuse, and the potential for profiling by U.S. authorities. The 2004 agreement was annulled in May 2006 on a technicality, and an interim agreement was provisionally agreed. . . .

Terrorist Finance Tracking Program (SWIFT). The Society for Worldwide Interbank Financial Telecommunication (SWIFT) is a Belgium-based syndicate of international banks, which started sharing large amounts of its processed data with the U.S. after 9/11 for the purposes of tracking terrorists' finances. When media reports revealed the existence of this program in 2006, the European Data Protection Supervisor ruled that the transfers breached EU data protection laws, and in February 2007, the European Parliament resolved that proposed U.S. improvements to the program were insufficient to adequately protect the personal data of EU citizens. U.S. negotiators were once again sent back to the drawing board. . . .

It was not until June 2010 that the European Commission was able to conclude a new draft agreement with Washington, and only with the inclusion of a number of new restrictions, including (1) oversight roles for both the European Commission and Europol to oversee the transfer of information and (2) limiting information requests to make them as narrow as possible.

Foreign Terrorist Organizations (FTOs). The EU's common definition of terrorism and designation of terrorist individuals and groups has acted as a powerful sanction against the free flow of terrorist finances. An individual or organization that is designated terrorist by both the EU and the U.S. is effectively being denied access to the world's biggest financial markets.

In 2005, Congress passed a bill urging the EU to add Hezbollah to the EU's wide-ranging list of terrorist organizations. The EU's refusal to proscribe Hezbollah as an FTO is impossible to understand. The Lebanon-based group is a radical transnational terrorist entity responsible for several acts of mass murder, especially against U.S. targets, including (1) the April 1983 bombing of the U.S. embassy in Beirut, which killed 63 people, including 17 Americans; (2) the October 1983 suicide truck bombing of a U.S. Marine barracks at Beirut airport, which killed 241; and (3) the 1996 Khobar Towers bombing in Saudi Arabia, which killed 19 U.S. servicemen. Hezbollah also serves as a terrorist proxy for the Iranian government, which has ramped up its attacks on Israel in recent years.

The EU has been categorical in its condemnation of U.S. detention and renditions policies.

Europe's willingness to turn a blind eye to Hezbollah's activities in Europe, especially its extensive fund-raising efforts, is unconscionable. Hezbollah's "secretary general" Hassan Nasrallah recently stated that without European support "our funding [and] moral, political, and material support will . . . dry up."

The United States rightly considers Hezbollah "a direct and growing threat to the United States and Latin America." The EU should finally list Hezbollah as an FTO and effectively freeze Hezbollah's terrorist operations in Europe and erode one of its primary fund-raising bases.

A Struggle Over Values

Detention and Renditions Policy. The EU has been categorical in its condemnation of U.S. detention and renditions policies. In 2006, EU Counter-Terrorism Co-ordinator Gijs de Vries stated:

In the fight against terrorism popular support is critical, including among Muslims. The struggle against terrorism is first and foremost a conflict over values. To win the battle for hearts and minds our policies to combat terrorism must respect the rights and values we have pledged to defend, including the rights of prisoners. Abu Ghraib [a U.S. military prison in Iraq where detainees were tortured in 2003–4], Guantánamo [Bay, a U.S. military detention facility in Cuba that is often accused of human rights violations] and CIA renditions have damaged America's standing in the world and have compromised our common struggle against terrorism. Credibility matters. The European Union continues to believe that in this battle we should be guided by established international legal standards, including international human rights law. Any war paradigm should operate within these standards.

In November 2005, the *Washington Post* and *Financial Times* published reports stating that the U.S. Central Intelligence Agency (CIA) was operating covert detention facilities in central and eastern Europe, where terrorist suspects were being interned without charge and then rendered to third countries for the purposes of torture. In January 2006, the European Parliament set up a 46-member committee to investigate these allegations, pledging to leave "no stone unturned" in their yearlong investigation to find out whether or not the CIA had used European countries to transport and illegally detain terrorist suspects. Poland and Romania were identified as alleged host countries of the U.S. detention facilities, and EU Commissioner Franco Frattini warned them that their voting rights in the European Council would be suspended if they were found guilty of hosting any such facilities.

In December 2005, U.S. Secretary of State Condoleezza Rice made a detailed speech to clarify the [George W. Bush] administration's policy on rendition, and U.S. Attorney General Alberto Gonzales met with Commissioner Frattini in Vienna in May 2006 to personally reassure him that the U.S.

neither tortured nor was complicit in the torture of suspects. Nevertheless, in its final report, the parliamentary committee concluded that the "excesses" of "the so-called 'war on terror,'" have produced, "a serious and dangerous erosion of human rights and fundamental freedoms."

No statement has been issued to clarify this position in light of reports that CIA sites in Europe could have played a key role in the successful operation against [al Qaeda leader] Osama bin Laden in May 2011, which EU presidents Herman Van Rompuy and José Manuel Barroso said in a joint statement "makes the world a safer place."

Recommendations

To achieve a cooperative EU-U.S. relationship in counterterrorism, I would recommend the following policies to the EU:

- *The European Parliament should approve the 2007 EU-U.S. PNR agreement without modification.* The EU should also consider extending the agreement for an additional seven years in light of the substantial evidence supporting its critical role in countering terrorism.

- *The current EU-U.S. negotiations to adopt an umbrella agreement on data sharing should accept U.S. data privacy standards as adequate.* An umbrella agreement should not seek to limit future agreements by restricting how and when information can be used, or imposing onerous monitoring requirements.

- *The EU should add Hezbollah to its list of foreign terrorist organizations.* The EU and the U.S. should coordinate their FTO lists as closely as possible, and the EU should add Hezbollah as a designated terrorist entity.

- *EU member states should exclude foreign-born individuals who engage in terrorist activities.* If a foreign-born individual is convicted of a terrorist offense in one EU member state, s/he should thereafter be excluded from all EU member states.

China Uses the War on Terror to Repress Uighur Separatist Movements

Chien-peng Chung

Chien-peng Chung is assistant professor of politics at Lingnan University in Hong Kong. In the following viewpoint, he argues that China used the September 11, 2001, al Qaeda terrorist attacks on the United States as a propaganda opportunity. He says that China began to characterize its opposition to Muslim Uighur separatist movements and to other ethnic movements as part of the War on Terror. By doing so, he suggests, China makes repression and human rights violations more palatable to both domestic and international audiences.

As you read, consider the following questions:

1. According to Chung, how did the United States show its sympathy for China's "Strike Hard"?
2. The Chinese government fears zealous religiosity for what reason, according to Chung?
3. Why does Chung say that the Chinese government is reluctant to play up the issue of terrorism?

Chien-peng Chung, "Confronting Terrorism and Other Evils in China: All Quiet on the Western Front?," *China and Eurasia Forum Quarterly*, vol. 4, no. 2, 2006. All rights reserved. Reprinted by permission.

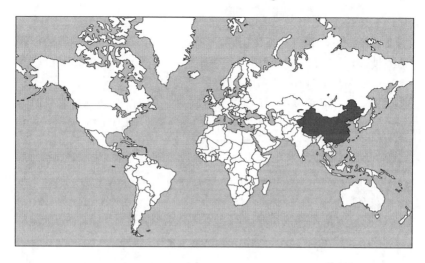

Terrorism is a difficult term to define in any context. It seems even more vague and broad when applied to circumstances in China, where any premeditated and violent criminal act against any person or property with the intent of spreading fear or causing harm for a political purpose, whether executed individually or by a group of people, would count as terrorism. The PRC [People's Republic of China] government is working on an antiterrorism law, which when promulgated, might provide an exact definition of terrorism. In any case, terrorism in China is usually identified with the East Turkestan Islamic Movement (ETIM) and other Uighur separatist cells in Xinjiang, and to a lesser extent, militant members of the Tibetan Buddhist clergy agitating for independence. Beijing is understandably concerned that a volatile Xinjiang would threaten import of oil and gas through pipelines from Kazakhstan in central Asia across Xinjiang to the Chinese coast, a restless Tibet would stoke the issue of legitimacy of Chinese rule, and a twitchy Inner Mongolia might damage China's relations with Mongolia.

War on Terror as Excuse

In the aftermath of the events of September 11, 2001 [that is, the 9/11 terrorist attacks on the United States], the PRC authorities treated the global "war on terror" essentially as a foreign relations exercise, to protect its relations with the United States, and as an excuse to crackdown on what it deemed to be terrorist activities on Chinese soil and uncover foreign linkages to the perpetrators. Washington has since become more sympathetic to Beijing's charge of terrorists fomenting "splittist" or separatist violence and its "Strike Hard" (*yan da*) campaign against them, most notably by placing the little-known ETIM on the U.S. list of terrorist organizations in August 2002. The PRC authorities have made much of 12 Uighur "terrorists" who joined the Taliban [an Islamic Afghan militant group] and are detained by the U.S. at its facilities at Guantánamo Bay [a U.S. military detention base in Cuba]. They have also accused another Uighur "terrorist" group, the East Turkestan Liberation Organization, of killing a Chinese embassy diplomat in Kyrgyzstan's Bishkek in 2002 and nineteen Chinese passengers in a China-bound Kyrgyz bus in 2003. Occasional reports have surfaced of Uighur separatists operating with the al Qaeda, Islamic Movement of Uzbekistan (IMU), Hizb ut-Tahrir, Chechens, and other groups in central Asia that use violence to pursue their aims, and even an IMU cell established in Xinjiang, but there has so far been no concrete proof.

The "three evils" offer rather good mass media propaganda for the PRC government to keep ethnic demands on the defensive.

Thus 9/11 should not be read as a demarcation or signpost in China's "war on terror," but should instead be recognized as an ongoing domestic affair reaching back years. Violent demonstrations for democracy and independence in Inner Mongolia in 1989 and 1990 were handled by armed police units, resulting in several fatalities. China's counterterrorist efforts started in Xinjiang with a confrontation between the police and armed rioters at Baren County in 1990, followed by violent events such as bombings of buses and public buildings, and gun attacks on policemen and officials, with the most fatalities occurring in a clash between soldiers and protestors in Yining City in 1997. PRC authorities have admitted to very few incidents in Xinjiang since the turn of 1997 and 1998, after the introduction of *yan da*, which started as a nationwide campaign to strike at skyrocketing crime, but has targeted separatism and illegal religious activities in Xinjiang principally but also in Tibet. Major rounds of demonstrations by protesting monks and nuns in Tibet started in 1987, but the last of them was dispersed by the authorities in 1993. This was shortly after the appointment of the uncompromising Chen Kuiyuan as Chinese Communist Party (CCP) secretary for Tibet, who banned all displays of the images of the self-exiled Dalai Lama, head of the Tibetan Buddhist hierarchy, after Beijing replaced his choice of the number two Panchen Lama with its own candidate in 1995. There have been occasional small-scale bombings since then—a bomb exploded outside a Lhasa police building in 1998 injuring four people and one in 2000 went off beside a Lhasa courthouse—but no mass risings.

Terrorism and the "Three Evils"

Terrorist or violent political acts are a manifestation of root causes that suppression alone does not adequately deal with. Also, as with elsewhere, terrorism in China cannot be understood in isolation. It has to be seen in the wider context, since the term "terrorist" is usually applied to separatist and unofficial religious groups in the ethnic autonomous regions of Xinjiang, Tibet, and to a lesser extent, Inner Mongolia. In Beijing's parlance, terrorism constitutes one of "three evils," together with separatism and religious fundamentalism, which, in its view, are all interconnected threats to China's national security and regional stability. This is because Beijing sees terrorism as a violent expression of the aim of ethnic separatism and the result of zealous religiosity on the part of minorities that threaten to displace the state as an object of adulation. As such, separatist-cum-religious terrorism is closely associated with the fears, grievances and aspirations of certain, though by no means most, ethnic minorities in China. The presence of the "three evils" also means that the root causes of terrorism—religious freedom, cultural autonomy, living standards, and political rights of ethnic minorities—are not addressed directly or earnestly enough by the Chinese authorities. Indeed, an unstated source of ethnic discontent is the discriminatory practices in the execution of minority policies of the PRC government, even assuming the purest intent.

Terrorism and Propaganda

For all their collective malfeasance, it must be admitted that the "three evils" offer rather good mass media propaganda for the PRC government to keep ethnic demands on the defensive, dismiss foreign scrutiny, encourage or support the causes of Chinese minorities, and perhaps most importantly, sustain the unity of China's dominant Han Chinese ethnicity. The last aspect is shaping up to be of increasing salience to China's leadership, in the face of the end of the state's socialist ideology [in the last 20 years, China has moved away from government control of the economy and toward a free market system] and the homogenizing, materialistic and individualistic effects of globalization, to prevent the emergence of centrifugal southern, provincial or coastal nationalisms that would challenge, or at least weaken, the present hegemonic state constructed around the ruling CCP, patriotic state-nationalism and a principal ethnic group.

Both the PRC authorities and émigré Uighur and Tibetan independence advocacy groups are carefully crafting a fine balance between playing up and playing down the threat of separatist violence. For Beijing, playing up the issue would discourage foreign trade and investments in Xinjiang or Tibet, but playing it down would deprive the authorities of excuses to initiate actions against separatists and religious radicals. For the émigré activists, the problem is either discrediting their cause by associating it with terrorism, or demonstrating their hopeless lack of influence in rousing their fellow minorities in China. However, even if the true state of separatist violence or terrorism is between an exaggeration and an understatement for both parties, it is far from being a phantom menace. China's western front has been mostly quiet for at least the past eight years now, but disturbances by ethnic minorities can recur with little forewarning.

The US War on Terror Should Be Fought with Intelligence, Not Military Force

Sara Daly

Sara Daly is a CIA counterterrorism analyst. In the following viewpoint, she argues that terrorism in the United States should be fought with intelligence, not military might. She claims that America has the military strength to crush the enemy, but terrorism is a fight that requires finding an enemy in a boundless battlefield. Most police are generally already aware of the activities of extremist groups and can therefore aid in the capture and prevention of terrorists and terrorist activities.

As you read, consider the following questions:

1. Why does the author believe calling on the military to battle terrorism is not a successful strategy?
2. What is one strategy mentioned in the viewpoint that can give local police the "upper hand" on fighting terrorists?
3. According to the author, is solid police work crucial to preventing future terrorist attacks?

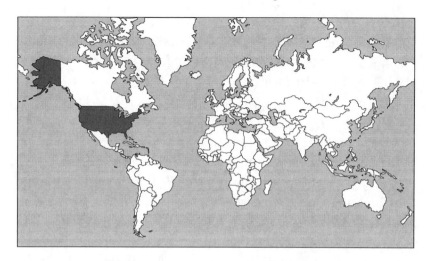

In this season of code-orange alerts, good intelligence rather than military might is the best way to protect our homeland. Information gathering is the most powerful weapon in the struggle to dismantle terrorist networks and prevent attacks.

The United States and other nations are hunting down small and often unconnected groups and individuals who hide their identities and surface only briefly to carry out terrorist attacks.

The terrorists are, by definition, in the business of terrorizing us, and want to make us feel helpless and hopeless in the face of their attacks.

Focus on Intelligence, Not Military Might

Much emphasis in the fight against terrorism has been placed on military capabilities. We have come to expect that planes, tanks, helicopters, and heavily armed soldiers will be used to protect America and defeat our enemies.

But calling out the Army, Air Force, Navy, and Marines in full battle gear to combat terrorism on a day-to-day basis is rarely a successful strategy at home or abroad. There's no question America has the military might to crush an enemy on the battlefield—but in fighting terrorism, the primary challenge is finding the enemy on a battlefield that has no boundaries.

If the job is done right, successful prevention of terrorism depends on gathering accurate information and stopping something from happening—often without public awareness. It is only the failure to prevent attacks that is felt, and along with it a profound sense that we are ultimately powerless to protect ourselves.

The terrorists are, by definition, in the business of terrorizing us, and want to make us feel helpless and hopeless in the face of their attacks. They want us to believe attacks come randomly and without warning, so that we don't even try to predict the unpredictable. They hope that by making us adopt defeatism as a philosophy, they can defeat us.

In most cases, the police are already aware of the activities of local extremist groups with established records of advocating and carrying out violent acts, and often know the players involved because of their past participation in terrorist activity.

Similar Patterns

In fact, there is plenty we have done and can do to combat terrorism. Recent terrorist events perpetrated by al Qaeda and Islamic extremist groups sympathetic to al Qaeda have similar patterns that can be identified by intelligence agencies working hand in glove with local police and security services in the US and around the world.

One of these recent patterns is for al Qaeda to devolve more authority to local Islamic extremist groups in places like Morocco, Saudi Arabia, and Turkey to carry out attacks against US and allied targets.

The 2002 Bali Bombing in Indonesia

In the evening of October 12, 2002, two powerful bombs exploded at Paddy's Bar and the Sari Club in the tourist district of Kuta, Bali. The death toll amounted to 164 foreigners, mostly Australians, and 38 Indonesians. Many more were injured, and the material damage was immense. These events left everyone on the otherwise tranquil Hindu island in shock, local inhabitants and visitors alike. The police accused the militant Islamist group Jemaah Islamiyah (JI) of carrying out the terrorist attacks. One of its leaders, Abu Bakar Ba'ashir, spent only about two years in prison, while another leader, Hambali (alias of Riduan Isamuddin), with allegedly close al Qaeda [an international terrorist organization] connections, was arrested in Thailand and is currently held in American custody. Three JI members were sentenced to death, and one to life imprisonment. Most notorious for his media performance was Amrozi bin Haji Nurhasyim who was defiant throughout the court hearings, smiling and giving himself the thumbs-up when his death sentence was read out loud. Imam Samudra, too, showed no remorse. . . . On November 9, 2008, . . . Imam Samudra, Amrozi, and Mukhlas [Huda bin Abdul Haq] were executed by firing squad.

Tineke Hellwig and Eric Tagliacozzo, eds.,
The Indonesia Reader: History, Culture, Politics.
Durham, NC: Duke University Press, 2009, p. 429.

In some cases, the individuals involved in the attacks are unknown to local police—al Qaeda often seeks out anonymous individuals. But in other cases, the individuals responsible for attacks are known to the police in the areas where they operate and have a history of terrorist activity. Al Qaeda relies on these more experienced operatives to pull off a successful attack.

This is where the local police can play the most crucial role in preventing future attacks. In most cases, the police are already aware of the activities of local extremist groups with established records of advocating and carrying out violent acts, and often know the players involved because of their past participation in terrorist activity.

Making Terrorists' Jobs Harder

Monitoring the activities of local extremists in individual countries—such as travel in and out of the country and involvement in criminal enterprises—can be carried out through physical surveillance and other methods of monitoring permissible under legal boundaries. This can give local police the upper hand.

By doing this, law enforcement agents will not be able to prevent every terrorist attack, but they will make terrorists' jobs a lot harder by dismantling networks and fostering a hostile operating environment. We know from past experience that faced with this situation, terrorists will either cease conducting attacks in that location and re-strategize, or move their operations completely.

Solid police work is crucial not only in following up on leads after an attack has occurred, but also in preventing future attacks. Efforts by police to identify operational patterns and the individuals in communities involved in terrorist activity will go a long way toward undermining terrorists' ability to instill a sense of randomness and fear.

The "war" on terrorism is really more comparable to the long and continuing battle against crime waged by police departments around the world. The leading role in this antiterrorism battle isn't played by GI Joe, but by Dick Tracy.

In Afghanistan and Pakistan, Improving Women's Rights Helps in the War on Terror

Charles M. Sennott

Charles M. Sennott is the vice president, executive editor, and cofounder of GlobalPost. In the following viewpoint, he reports how women and mothers in Afghanistan and Pakistan often work for peace and against terrorist indoctrination. He discusses especially the efforts of Mossarat Qadeem—an academic, mother, and peace activist who is striving to empower mothers to work against terrorism. Sennott suggests that empowering and educating mothers can help to weaken radical Islamist groups, such as the Taliban, and may be a major force in the fight against terrorism in Pakistan and Afghanistan.

As you read, consider the following questions:

1. According to Sennott, what resentments and angers do the Taliban recruiters exploit?
2. What is the Institute for Inclusive Security, according to Sennott?
3. How does Sennott say that Qadeem has been threatened?

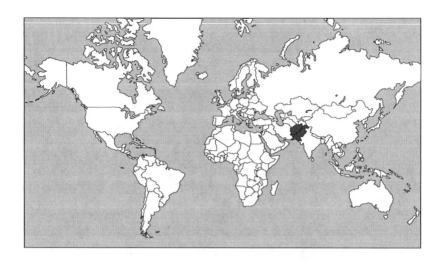

In Peshawar, Pakistan, the sermons of radical imams are carried on loudspeakers atop the minarets of mosques, and the words echo in the narrow streets.

Women Against Terrorism

The Pakistani Taliban [a radical Islamic group] is strong in Peshawar. In recent months, the Taliban leadership has used these radical sermons to step up recruitment of young fighters in their jihad against the Pakistani government and across the border in Afghanistan.

The Taliban recruiters are playing off bitter resentments over the Pakistani military's offensive that has left millions displaced. The Taliban also exploit anger over America's escalation of the war in Afghanistan, using it to search for young men willing to kill in the name of God.

A 16-year-old boy from a small village in the Khyber Agency near Peshawar answered the Taliban's call and the militants set about grooming him to be a suicide bomber.

He underwent a rigorous indoctrination and was trained to "accept martyrdom," to borrow the language used, at the ready to detonate a belt bomb to kill [himself] and as many Pakistani soldiers and civilians as possible.

But there was one problem. The boy's mother, Zubida, found out about her son's plans. She knew her son had been led to a place in his faith that strayed far from who he was and the lessons she had taught him growing up about Islam's message of tolerance and respect for life.

Zubida, whose last name is not being used to protect her identity, turned to Mossarat Qadeem, an academic turned peace activist and a mother herself, who has established a center in Peshawar that empowers women in the struggle against terrorism.

Qadeem, who attended a recent conference by the Institute for Inclusive Security at Harvard University's John F. Kennedy School of Government, says she is now working to "re-integrate" and "re-educate," as she puts it, 82 young men who've come forward through the women in their lives.

Typically it is young men who have been encouraged to come forward by mothers like Zubida. They are in some cases turned over to authorities by their mothers with promises that they will be given an opportunity to return to society and break free from the process of radicalization and militancy that is pushed by the local Taliban leaders.

Qadeem told me her story on Jan. 12 [2010] at the Harvard University conference, which was coordinated by the chair of the Institute for Inclusive Security, Ambassador Swanee Hunt.

"We have to work to reclaim our faith," said Qadeem. "The mothers of these young men are a very important part of succeeding in that."

The institute uses research, training and advocacy to promote the inclusion of all community stakeholders, particularly women, in pursuing peace. The weeklong conference brought together leading female academics, parliamentarians, human rights activists and journalists from Iran, Lebanon, Bosnia,

Rwanda and Pakistan to share their experiences and shed light on the unique role women play in resolving conflict.

Qadeem told me how Zubida, the mother of the 16-year-old boy intent on being a suicide bomber, had reached out to her in December [2009], saying, "My boy is not a Talib, but the Taliban have taken him away. He has been indoctrinated by them."

Qadeem worked with Zubida to bring her son out of hiding and to turn him over to the authorities.

Women Ending Violence

"We have to work to reclaim our faith," said Qadeem. "The mothers of these young men are a very important part of succeeding in that."

When the young men turn themselves in, Qadeem explained, they take the dramatic step of surrendering to Pakistani counterterrorism officials who question them and also provide psychological counseling and religious education aimed at countering the Taliban's warped and violent interpretations of the Koran, explains Qadeem.

A political science professor at the University of Peshawar, Qadeem said she has turned away from academia to start an organization known by the acronym PAIMAN, which means "promise" in Pashto. The organization works to empower Pakistani women to counter Islamic militancy and to pursue conflict resolution in their communities.

"We are doing critical analysis of the role women can play in ending violence and extremism," said Qadeem. "We are trying to develop the need for peace from within as an instrument to end violence."

She said she had offered direct training to some 5,000 women through the Peshawar-based organization which has 18 offices around the country and more than 200 staff. Those women in turn have developed as leaders in their community to "teach peace" and, Qadeem said, have spread the message to some 75,000 additional women.

Qadeem operates in what she describes as "a very insecure environment." She is on the hit list of two Taliban groups in the Khyber Agency, and has been repeatedly threatened in her work. So why does she do it?

"The vulnerability of my youths keeps me awake at night and the killing of the innocent people every day bleeds my heart. As a daughter of the soil, I am trying to use our community's network of women to break the hold of militancy on their sons and brothers and husbands. That is an important avenue to achieving real peace."

Periodical and Internet Sources Bibliography

The following articles have been selected to supplement the diverse views presented in this chapter.

Basil Fernando	"Indonesia: Police Act Disproportionately in War on Terror—Unarmed Suspects Shot Dead," Asian Human Rights Commission, May 17, 2010. www.humanrights.asia.
Patrick Gallahue	"A Worrying Front in the War on Drugs," *Guardian*, June 6, 2010.
Ernest Harsch	"Africa Looks Beyond 'War on Terror,'" *Africa Renewal*, October 2009.
George Jones	"Blair to Curb Human Rights in War on Terror," *Telegraph*, August 6, 2005.
Nicholas D. Kristof	"China and Terrorism," *New York Times*, April 29, 2008.
Laura MacInnis	"U.S. 'War on Terror' Eroded Rights Worldwide: Experts," Reuters, February 16, 2009. www.reuters.com.
Sally McNamara	"The EU-U.S. Counterterrorism Relationship: An Agenda for Cooperation," Heritage Foundation, March 8, 2011. www.heritage.org.
Abigail Salisbury	"Human Rights and the War on Terror in Ethiopia," JURIST, August 2, 2011. http://jurist.org.
Michael Schmidt	"The New American Imperialism in Africa," Anarkismo.net, January 22, 2007. www.anarkismo.net.
Ben Terrall	"Funding Indonesia's Abusive Military," *In These Times*, September 26, 2007.

GLOBALVIEWPOINTS

Government Responses to Terrorist Attacks

Like Norway, the United Kingdom Should Learn to React Calmly to Terrorist Attacks

Iain Macwhirter

Iain Macwhirter is a Scottish political commentator. In the following viewpoint, he argues that Norway reacted with calm and unity to a deadly terrorist attack in 2011. Macwhirter argues that Norway is a strong democracy, and so reacted in a measured way. He adds that terrorists thrive on repressive measures that inflame hatred. He says that, in contrast, Britain's reaction to terrorist attacks in 2005 was excessive and repressive. He argues that in the future, Britain should model its response to terror on Norway's.

As you read, consider the following questions:

1. What did Prime Minister Stoltenberg say was the Norwegian response to democracy?

2. According to Macwhirter, some say the Norwegian response was measured because of what characteristics of the terrorist Breivik?

3. What does Macwhirter suggest may have been the reason that Britain's response to terrorism in 2005 was more repressive than it had been in the past?

Iain Macwhirter, "Norway Showed Us the Way to Respond to Terrorism," *Herald Scotland*, July 31, 2011. Reprinted by permission.

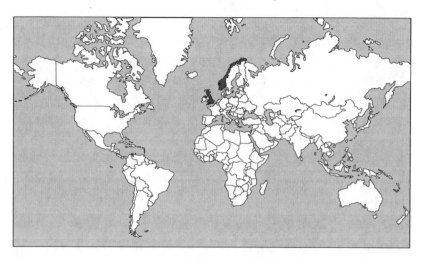

I wasn't going to write about the Norwegian massacre [in which a right-wing extremist killed sixty-nine people at a summer camp], because it has rather fallen from the front pages—then I realised that was precisely the point.

Terrorism, but No Censorship

Had it been the al Qaeda [a militant Islamic terrorist group] atrocity that many initially suspected, things would have been different. Today's press would have been dominated by commentary about "Norway's 9/11" and the "new Nordic front in the war on terror". We would be told there was now "nowhere to hide" from Islamist fanatics.

As it happened, of course, this was not an act of Islamic fundamentalist terror, but Christian fundamentalist terror. Commentators and newspaper editors have been embarrassed, particularly, the *Daily Mail*'s Melanie Phillips, whose columns were cited in Anders Behring Breivik's [the terrorist-shooter in the incident] "manifesto". Mind you, the *Independent*'s Robert Fisk was once cited by Osama bin Laden [al Qaeda's leader], which just goes to show that you can't always be sure the right people agree with you when you write opinionated commentary.

But there were no calls for censorship of right-wing views, or any crackdown in Norway against the anti-immigration parties. Norway provided a textbook demonstration of how a civilised country should respond to these rare and random acts of unspeakable barbarity—with stoicism and measure. Despite having been the prime target of the Oslo bombing, the Norwegian Prime Minister, Jens Stoltenberg, avoided the temptation to declare another pointless "war on terror" or promulgate an agenda of repressive measures to "protect the people".

A repressive response is precisely what the terrorist wants because it engenders hate between communities.

Instead he turned this tragic event into a chance to unite the country, celebrate liberal values and heal divisions. "The Norwegian response to violence is more democracy, more openness and greater political participation," he said. The people took his lead, and mounted huge peaceful demonstrations holding flowers to show their respect for the dead and their commitment to their values. Unfortunately, that isn't as newsworthy as a war on terror, so Norway slipped into the foreign news pages.

Compare Britain's response to 7/7 in 2005 [attacks on London's transportation system that killed fifty-two people on July 7, 2005]. Within days, then Home Secretary, Charles Clarke, under pressure from [Prime Minister] Tony Blair and the *Sun*, had put together an agenda of repressive legislation. Top of the list was 90-day detention for terrorists and the outlawing of what was called "indirect incitement to terrorism"— the nearest Britain has come to legislating against thought crime. The 90-day detention plan was dropped after it was realized this could mean suspects receiving the equivalent of a six-month prison sentence, with remission, without being charged with any offence. But Blair had no qualms about abolishing the thousand-year-old right of habeas corpus—the right not to be held without charge.

Terrorists Want Repression

A repressive response is precisely what the terrorist wants because it engenders hate between communities. In Chris Morris's brilliant satire on religious terrorism, *Four Lions*, one of the suicide bombers insists they should target the local mosque. That way, peaceful Muslims would be roused to anger against the "kuffar" (nonbelievers), the government would crack down on them and there would be a religious civil war hastening "the end of days".

If only, after 9/11 [the September 11, 2001, al Qaeda attack on the United States], George W Bush had appealed for calm and urged citizens to hold firm to their democratic values. Instead he promised to get bin Laden "dead or alive", declared war on international terror, and then invaded Iraq, a country that had no connection whatever to al Qaeda. In doing so, he played right into bin Laden's hands, igniting a furious response throughout the Middle East to the illegal invasion of a nominally Muslim country.

Of course, there are those who say it was only because Breivik was a "Christian" bomber rather than a Muslim one, that the response was so responsible. Aren't far-right groups on the march already in northern Europe? The Freedom Party in Holland, the Sweden Democrats, the True Finns. The *Arab News* last week [in July 2011] slammed the West for hypocrisy, saying the Norway shooting was played down because it didn't fit the "racist" mould of "Islamic terrorism".

There may be an element of truth in that. Certainly, UK papers which had prematurely pronounced the massacre as the work of al Qaeda, curiously became less interested after it was discovered the perpetrator was white and right-wing.

But if the killer had fitted that profile, I don't believe the Norwegian response would have been markedly different. The

7/7 London Bombings

Three improvised explosive devices (IED) exploded on London Underground trains shortly after 8:50 a.m. on July 7, 2005, within about 50 seconds of each other. The fourth IED exploded on a double-decker bus in Tavistock Square, less than a kilometer from King's Cross mainline station at 9:47 a.m., some 57 minutes after the three underground devices were initiated.

The trains were carrying approximately 800 persons and on two of the trains which were on the Circle line, seven persons died in both the Circle line explosions. On one Circle line train the device exploded in a section of shallow subsurface tunnel and blew through a dividing wall hitting a train passing in the opposite direction. The third train which was on the Piccadilly line was in a more confined tunnel, about 70 feet (21.3 m) underground, with 25 persons dead and several hundred injured. This deep tunnel explosion damaged the structural integrity of the tunnel itself, which hampered rescue and forensic investigations. In all three trains the devices were initiated in the standing area within the double doors of the carriage and were located in the front carriage in the two Circle line trains and in the forward section of the second carriage in the Piccadilly line train.

The fourth device in the bus devastated the upper area of the bus killing 13 and injuring 30 or more.

Frances L. Edwards and Friedrich Steinhäusler, eds.,
NATO and Terrorism: On Scene: New Challenges
for First Responders and Civil Protection.
Dordrecht, The Netherlands: Springer, 2006, pp. 88–89.

security services and the Norwegian police—who were heavily criticised for their delayed reaction to the events—might have stepped up security at immigration points and known Muslim extremists might have been questioned. But there would have been nothing like the British reaction to 7/7.

So, why has Norway reacted so calmly? Let's put it the other way: Why was Britain's first reaction a repressive one? Britain is a phlegmatic country with firm values, not unlike Norway. For three decades, Britain took the IRA [an Irish terrorist group] terror bombings in its stride and even [former prime minister] Margaret Thatcher, a target of the IRA Brighton bombing in 1984, never proposed detention without trial on the British mainland. Why was Britain so different in 2005?

Perhaps the presence of Rupert Murdoch [a major international tabloid publisher], the "24th member of Blair's cabinet" according to former Number 10 [Downing Street, the prime minister's residence] staffer Lance Price, might have had something to do with it. Blair was obsessed with pleasing the tabloid press. In Norway, they don't allow foreign proprietors to dictate government policy. But more importantly, Norway is a small, robust and relatively homogeneous community, used to adversity, and confident in itself and its democracy. Belligerence is a sign of weakness. Let's hope political leaders learn from Norway's example, because we will probably be here again.

Russia Struggles to Find the Correct Response to Terror Attacks

Sergei Roy

Sergei Roy is a Moscow-based journalist. In the following viewpoint, he argues that following suicide bombings in March 2010, many Russian people and officials called for severe crackdowns on potential terrorists. Roy notes that the actual response from the government has been more measured, however. He says it has included acknowledging a massive failure of security as well as measures intended to deal with the social and ideological roots of terrorism. He suggests that the fears of state repression are exaggerated.

As you read, consider the following questions:

1. Why does Roy say the reaction to the terrorist bombing was more acute in Moscow?

2. What does Roy believe will be the only practical result of the calls for tougher legislative and executive measures?

3. What forceful expression does Roy say President Medvedev made in the aftermath of the blasts?

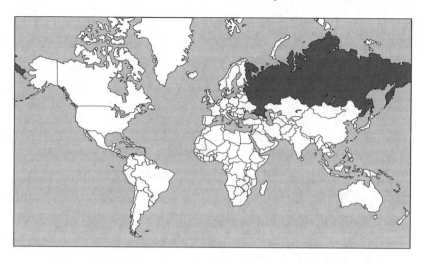

The immediate responses to the Metro bombings in Moscow [referring to the suicide bombings in March 2010 that killed forty people] were on the whole predictable and predictably varied.

Security Failures

The population at large, particularly in Moscow and especially on the Internet, gave vent to anger against the authorities, particularly the FSB [the Russian Federal Security Service] and the police, for their failure to protect them against the murderous attacks. The reaction was all the more acute as the people of Moscow had not known such tragedies for six years and now realized, without saying so aloud, that they themselves had grown complacent, happy-go-lucky, and irresponsible in matters of public safety and vigilance, especially in such "soft" targets as the Metro.

In the heat of the moment some members of the public expressed the desire to drive all the natives of the Caucasus now living in or coming to Moscow and elsewhere in Russia back to the North Caucasus republics and fence them off with razor wire, etc. Of course, there was an immediate response to these angry outbursts from the more sober-minded element:

Such measures were clearly impracticable and in fact plain stupid, amounting as they did to creating a mini Afghanistan on Russia's borders. [Russia fought a long, costly war to control Afghanistan in the 1980s.] A leaf we've turned over.

The official reaction from the two agencies most concerned, the FSB and interior ministry, was one of admitting abject failure. The suicidal "black widows" [that is, the female suicide bombers] were known to these agencies; their disappearance, after the death of their bandit husbands, to some training camp or base for suicide bombers should have been acted upon; they could have been stopped as they traveled to Moscow by coach if the checks en route had been less perfunctory or carried out at all; their appearance at a rented flat in Moscow could have been noticed if the police officers responsible for the area had been more diligent. And so on. The public has maliciously commented that all this could have been done if the police had not been too busy pursuing more lucrative activities like pestering petty tradesmen.

President Medvedev, after some forceful expressions in the immediate aftermath of the blasts . . . came up with a sensible five-point program.

On the political scene, inside and outside of Parliament there was a natural tendency to keep in tune with the public mood. Hence the calls for tougher legislative and executive measures to combat extremism, including some exotic ones, like the fingerprinting of everyone from the North Caucasus, lifting the moratorium on capital punishment, and the like. This sort of talk can be safely predicted to gradually fizzle out and bear no practical result except perhaps for President [Dmitry] Medvedev's proposal to pass legislation providing for stiffer sentences for complicity in terrorist acts.

Angry Rhetoric and Practical Measures

On the right-hand side of the political spectrum (which is here entirely extra-parliamentary) and in the media . . . , there was a reflex fear expressed that the powers-that-be will immediately "tighten the screws," curtail democratic freedoms, especially the freedom of the press. All of this was not just predictable but outright boring, as these fringe elements trundle out the same hate-ridden nonsense each time something tragic happens in this land. No wonder their electoral support is in the statistical error category. How else is the public to react, say, to the argument that the poor terrorists were blowing up innocent people merely in an attempt to draw attention to the unbearable situation in the Caucasus? And that's just a sample of this kind of lunacy.

President Medvedev, after some forceful expressions in the immediate aftermath of the blasts (like "We will destroy them all"), came up with a sensible five-point program involving the state's political and economic structures, the public, religious and culture figures and educationalists, intended to deal with the social and ideological roots of terrorism.

In this spirit, my understanding is that the fight against the worldwide jihadist scourge will be with us for decades to come. It calls for unity, vigilance, and even sacrifices, both within the nation and internationally. Just how attainable these desiderata are is another matter.

Germany May Institute Full-Body Scanners in Airports in Response to a Terrorist Attack

Spiegel

Spiegel is a German newspaper. In the following viewpoint, it reports that a failed terrorist attack on an airplane bound for the United States has made German officials reconsider a controversial security scanner. The full-body scanner allows security personnel to do a digital strip search and see through passengers' clothes to determine whether they are concealing weapons. Spiegel speculates that such scanners might have foiled the terrorist attack on the American airplane, where the terrorist concealed explosives in his underwear. Nonetheless, the German government is still hesitant to use the scanners because of privacy concerns.

As you read, consider the following questions:

1. According to *Spiegel*, what does the full-body scanner use to produce an image of the human body, and what can it reveal?

2. Why didn't Umar Farouk Abdulmutallab pass through Amsterdam customs, according to *Spiegel*?

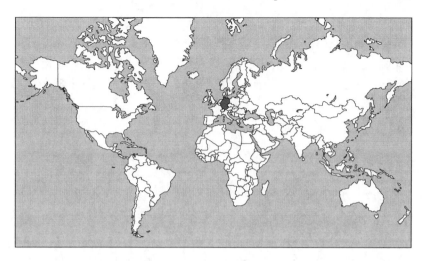

3. How does *Spiegel* say that American officials resolve privacy issues related to the full-body scanner?

The political fallout from Friday's [December 25, 2009] attempted terror attack [by Umar Farouk Abdulmutallab, who concealed a bomb in his underwear] on Northwest Airlines Flight 253 from Amsterdam to Detroit continued on Wednesday. While American President Barack Obama criticized national security services for not spotting would-be terrorist Umar Farouk Abdulmutallab earlier, the debate in Europe has focused on airport security. After expressing initial opposition to controversial new security measures like what Germans are calling the "*nacktscanner*" or "naked scanner," some German politicians are now saying that full-body scanners may soon be installed in German airports as well.

Abdulmutallab Would Have Been Caught

The full-body scanner uses high-frequency radio waves to produce an image of the human body. This means that anything hidden under clothes—ceramic weapons or explosives for example—is revealed. It also enables security officials with an alternative to pat-down body searches.

Still, the fact that the machines "see" underneath a passenger's clothes has led to concerns about intrusion on privacy and infringement of civil rights in both Europe and the United States. There have also been a slew of alarming descriptions of the security systems, like "striptease surveillance" and "digital strip search."

Interior Minister Thomas de Maizière . . . indicated he is more open to the full-body scanners than previously.

It is highly likely that, had Abdulmutallab passed through such a scanner, the explosives he had moulded to his inner thigh would have been detected. And in fact, such scanners are already in use at Amsterdam's Schiphol airport, where Abdulmutallab boarded the flight to Detroit. But as *NRC Handelsblad* reports Abdulmutallab never passed through Amsterdam customs because, as a transit passenger with a connecting flight, he technically never entered the Netherlands. He was simply subjected to another standard security check before boarding the flight to Detroit.

On Wednesday, the Dutch government announced at a press conference that within the next three weeks it would begin screening all US-bound passengers using full-body scanners. Debates over full-body scanners have simmered in the European Union [EU] for several years now. Although a pilot program is being tested by the Dutch government at Schiphol, the EU has been reluctant to permit mandatory use of the technology because it has the potential of taking nude images of passengers. Earlier this week, Schiphol spokesperson Mirjam Snoerwang told *NRC Handelsblad*, "European regulations tell us we can only put people through them (the full-body scanners) on a voluntary basis. And objections have been raised with regards to privacy." Several airports in the United Kingdom also have full-body scanners.

"Underwear Bomber," cartoon by David Donar, www.CartoonStock.com. Copyright © David Donar. Reproduction rights obtainable from www.CartoonStock.com.

German Interior Minister Reconsiders Scanners

Germany doesn't have any and, as late as Monday, German politicians were still saying that they didn't think full-body scanners were necessary. Now, though, in an interview with the daily *Süddeutsche Zeitung* published on Wednesday, Interior Minister Thomas de Maizière, a conservative Christian Democrat and member of Chancellor Angela Merkel's cabinet, indicated he is more open to the full-body scanners than previously. The interior ministry is responsible for border security and for protecting the country against terrorism. De Maizière's predecessor, Wolfgang Schäuble of the CDU [Christian Democratic Union], had said that "we will have nothing to do with this nonsense." But asked whether the government was planning an about-turn on previous policies, de Maizière told the newspaper that the full-body scanners were actually being tested even back when Schäuble was quoted on the subject. "The so-called 'nonsense' had to do—and still does—with the technical options available at the time and with the resulting pictures which did not take into account personal rights," de Maizière said.

And although in the interview, he appeared to be more open to seeing the scanners installed in German airports, de Maizière was also quick to point out that before they could be, three criteria needed to be fulfilled. "Firstly, any such equipment must be efficient, it must identify the things that one needs to identify," he said. "Secondly, the equipment must be completely harmless in terms of human health. And thirdly, it must comprehensively take into account an individual's rights." At the moment, de Maizière noted, "we are really only arguing about the third criteria. That discussion is appropriate—but all of the three criteria must be fulfilled. Only then can we make a decision about the installation of such devices."

The full-body scanner is currently being tested by Germany's federal police, who also have responsibility for airport security. The results of these tests are expected in mid-2010, after which full-body scanners may be installed in some German airports.

Potential health problems include the exposure of frequent travelers to radio frequencies. But as L-3 Communications, a company that makes a full-body scanner, told *Scientific American* magazine, the energy projected by the radio wave scanners is "one ten-thousandth the energy in a cell phone transmission."

In an interview with German radio station HR-Info, Professor Rolf Michel, the head of the [German] Commission on Radiological Protection which is part of Germany's environment ministry, warned against any airport scanners that use X-rays on humans. Long-term exposure could cause cancer, he said. And he also remained concerned about the full-body scanner, which uses radio waves rather than X-rays. "Up until now we have had little information as to whether these could be dangerous. The problem for us is that there is simply not enough information on the subject. At the moment there is intensive research under way to find out if we need to be worried about biological effects," he concluded.

Privacy Issues Remain Unresolved

Far more controversial at the moment, though, are privacy issues. And these are being resolved in a variety of ways. In American airports already using the scanners, security officials who are doing the scanning are in a different area from the passengers being scanned. There is no personal contact so that all they see are the outlines of the body and they never see the scanned individual's face. Images can also be discarded immediately after scanning.

It is also possible to blank out or blur the face of the scanned individual, and German police are experimenting with reducing the resulting pictures to mere outlines. Elsewhere tests are also being done which keeps human involvement to a minimum; instead a computer scans the images and alerts security officials if something unusual is found.

"Should these scanners be introduced, human dignity and the protection of individual rights must also be taken into account."

Aside from privacy issues the machine has several other drawbacks: It cannot detect any weapons or explosives concealed internally. This happened in the assassination attempt earlier in 2009 on the Saudi Arabian deputy minister of interior. His assailant, who died in the attempt, had concealed explosives in his anal cavity. Additionally, the full-body scanner apparently cannot see anything concealed under vinyl or plastic or anything that looks like skin, either.

The debate over the use of such scanners is far from over in Germany. Although the interior minister seemed more positive on Wednesday, Justice Minister Sabine Leutheusser-Schnarrenberger, a member of the Free Democrats (FDP) the CDU's junior coalition partner in the German government, remained more skeptical. In an interview with the daily *Berliner Zeitung*, she said that, "whether more technological controls could have stopped the attempted attack is only going to become clear once there has been a thorough investigation."

Germany's federal commissioner for data protection, Peter Schaar, agreed. Speaking to the same newspaper, Schaar said: "What surprises me is how quickly objections are being forgotten—and before basic questions (about the event) have even been answered. What needs to be explained is how the explosives were smuggled through the security controls and whether this technology could actually guard against this. Additionally, should these scanners be introduced, human dignity and the protection of individual rights must also be taken into account."

India's Response to Terrorism Has Been Complex and Effective

Ajit Doval

Ajit Doval is the former head of India's Intelligence Bureau. In the following viewpoint, he argues that India has used its democratic institutions and a focus on policing rather than military solutions to craft an effective counterterrorism program.

As you read, consider the following questions:

1. According to Doval, what has India's response been conditioned by besides its security interests?
2. What border control measures does Doval say India employed?
3. What developments in Bangladesh make handling terrorism more difficult, according to Doval?

Indian strategic response to terrorism has been a delicate blending of the hard and soft power of the state which, at times, invites snide comments like—a democracy that has room even for violence. Besides safeguarding national security interests, Indian response has been conditioned by its democratic polity, need to accommodate communal sensitivities

Ajit Doval, "Islamic Terrorism in South Asia and India's Strategic Response," *Policing: A Journal of Policy and Procedure.* Oxford University Press, 2007. All rights reserved. Reprinted by permission.

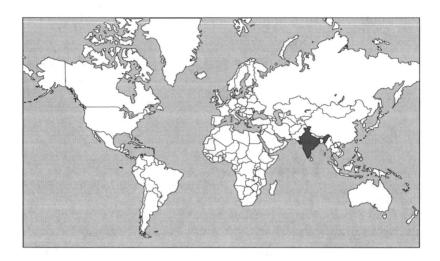

and safety of its citizens. The global and regional settings, complexity of relations with neighbouring countries and international obligations on terrorist fronts have also influenced the response. Moreover, India having long historical experience of grappling with civilizational conflicts, has conditioned the mind-set, both of the rulers and the ruled. India has traditionally avoided head-on collisions with civilizational adversaries and preferred conflict avoidance and conflict resolution, trying to contain physical confrontation at a low level. The high tolerance of Indian civil society and its ability to take losses in its stride is also a great national strength whose strategic import may not be obvious to a Western analyst.

De-linking Islam and Terror

One of the cornerstones of India's counterterrorist strategy has been to de-link Islam from terrorism and treat terrorists as a class devoid of any religious identity. Terrorist efforts to project themselves as soldiers of Islam and seize control of Muslim society through coercion and persuasion are sought to be defeated. To achieve this, communal polarization of the civil society on religious fault lines is prevented. Muslims are seen as victims of the phenomenon rather than its perpetrator. It was duly reflected in enactment and enforcement of laws, affirmative actions to redress genuine grievances, supporting liberal and pluralistic Islamic thought and political engagement of Muslims.

Democracy was used as an effective tool to fight terrorists. In Jammu and Kashmir [the northernmost state of India and the site of a long-standing dispute with neighbouring Pakistan], even at the height of terrorist violence with average killing figures as high as 3,000 a year, elections to state assembly were held in 1996 and 2002 (state assembly having a 6-year term) with an impressive turnout. Even parliamentary elections for the government in the center were held regularly along with the rest of the country. Terrorist resistance to holding of elections by unleashing violence against the party leaders, candidates and voters was resolutely countered. Successful holding of free and fair elections proved to be silent but a most effective display of civil societies' rejection of terrorists—both in terms of means and ends. As elected governments had a political interest in maintaining law and order and providing security to their voters, they became principal instruments of fighting terror unleashed by their co-religionists.

The next element of strategic response was dealing with terrorism as essentially a problem of policing and criminal administration rather than a military problem. The police forces which are locally recruited and belong to the same religious, ethnic, linguistic and social milieu were put on the lead role. The central forces whenever deployed were governed by the civilian laws and made answerable to the civilian judicial and administrative authorities. Infirmities of the police were made good through central assistance in training, equipment, intelligence, etc., and enhancing their strike capabilities by placing central forces at their disposal. . . . In Kashmir, the entire counterterrorist apparatus was placed under a unified headquarter headed by the elected chief minister. Local heads of army, police, and intelligence worked as its members and his advisors.

Strengthening of intelligence apparatus was accorded a high priority. Working on the doctrine that if you fail to surprise the terrorists you are in for surprises, intelligence operational capabilities were substantially increased. The country's Intelligence Bureau was designated as the nodal authority for counterterrorism. Aiming at seamless coordination, platforms like the Multi-Agency Centre and Joint Task Force on Intelligence, with representatives from all central and local security agencies, were created.

All solutions cannot be found exclusively through use of coercive power of the state. Political initiatives have to play a seminal role in complementing the security efforts.

Border Management

As both the terrorists and their hardware came to India from [the neighbouring countries of] Pakistan and Bangladesh, effective border management became an integral part of India's counterterrorist response. Access was sought to be denied to the intruders by erecting border fencing along Indo-Pak and Indo-Bangladesh borders complemented by border lighting, sensors and other technical devices. In addition, central forces were deployed on the borders to check infiltration. Though it did reduce the menace, it failed to eliminate it.

A major part of India's counterterrorist effort also centered around denying strategic targets to the terrorists and upgrading overall protective society. Specialized outfits were created for providing security to the Indian prime minister and other important threatened personalities. Strong anti-hijacking measures were taken and aviation security strengthened. While India achieved commendable success in denying strategic targets to the terrorists, it failed to provide full protection to common citizens. India's huge size, population of over 1.1 billion and a free democracy left some inevitable gaps which enabled the terrorists to strike.

While in security terms India pursues the objective of zero tolerance to terrorism, in political terms it also believes that all solutions cannot be found exclusively through use of coercive power of the state. Political initiatives have to play a seminal role in complementing the security efforts including exposure of diabolical designs of the terrorists and building a strong civil society support for governmental initiatives. India has kept its doors open for peace initiatives provided the violence was abjured. It politically engaged over ground separatist leaders in J&K [Jammu and Kashmir] to narrow down the differences and convince them of futility of violence. Over a period of time, it had a moderating effect.

Neutralizing collaborative networks of terrorists like gun runners, operators of funding channels, smugglers, organized crime syndicates, etc., figured high in India's response strategy. Intelligence-driven capabilities were developed to degrade these networks, most of them having transnational linkages.

Winning over the confidence of and energizing the vast Muslim majority which does not approve of the radicals . . . is vital for winning this battle.

Political Solutions to Terrorists

Tackling Pakistan, the primary exporter of terror to India, remained a high priority. Political and diplomatic pressures were exerted to make it abandon use of terrorism as an instrument of its state policy. Political engagements and initiation of confidence-building measures did help but not to the desired extent. There were serious gaps in what Pakistan promised and what it delivered.

With the fast radicalization of Afghanistan, Pakistan and Bangladesh on one hand and erosion in the will and capability of the governments in power there, the overall security scenario in the region stands highly vitiated. The Taliban's ground entrenchment, recruitments of new cadres, battle preparedness and an increase in drug-linked financial resources are a cause of concern. Bases in Pakistan make smothering of [international terrorist group] al Qaeda too distant a possibility. Drying up of accurate operational intelligence is reducing the tactical success rate of the troops. In Pakistan, sharp accretions in sectarian violence among competing radical groups, a growing hold of heavily armed terrorists in North-West Frontier Province and Balochistan and the credibility of the military regime [in Pakistan] at an all-time low have forced the government to play on the back foot. [Pakistani president Pervez] Musharraf's sharply declining popularity and tenuous control over levers of power, except army, may lead to political anarchy in this nuclearized Islamic state of which radical elements may emerge as the net beneficiaries. Bangladesh is passing through a highly unstable political phase and democracy has been held in abeyance with postponement of elections. The radicals who once stood totally discredited have staged a comeback with vengeance and mainstream political parties are increasingly finding that their support was indispensable to gain power.

India will have to maintain a high degree of vigil . . . in the wake of these developments. Further beefing up its intelligence capabilities will have to figure high in its priorities. The security agencies will have to be enabled, both materially and through legal empowerment to prevent and preempt terrorist strikes. As it can ill afford to suffer heavy casualties indefinitely, it will have to use all its political and diplomatic skills to prevail upon its neighbours to irretrievably roll back terrorist infrastructures in their countries. The pressure to hand over to India wanted terrorists who have taken shelter in these countries will also have to be pursued with renewed vigor.

Greater and more meaningful international cooperation in the fight against terrorism will also have to be achieved. New ideas and models of cooperation are necessary as the old ones have run out of their steam. Winning over the confidence of and energizing the vast Muslim majority which does not approve of the radicals but prefers to remain quiet about it is vital for winning this battle. From indifferent onlookers beyond the fence they will have to be made to play the role of front-line players. All this is doable.

India's Response to Terrorism Has Been Ineffectual

Ajai Sahni

Ajai Sahni is executive director of the Institute for Conflict Management in New Delhi and the editor of South Asia Intelligence Review. *In the following viewpoint, he argues that India has failed to craft theoretical or practical responses to terrorism. In particular, he argues that India makes apologies for terrorists, making it appear that terrorism is acceptable. He also argues that India's policing, military, and intelligence systems are deeply ineffectual in dealing with terrorist threats. He concludes that India badly needs reforms to confront terrorism.*

As you read, consider the following questions:

1. From what two factors does Sahni say terrorism draws strength?

2. What does the United Nations say should be the minimum police to population ratio, and how does it compare to India's police to population ratio, according to Sahni?

3. What statistics does Sahni use to show what he calls the military's acute and mounting crisis in leadership cadres?

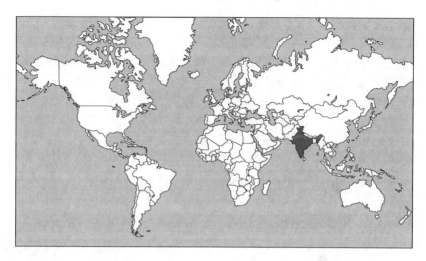

Despite apparent and often fierce condemnations of terrorism [in India], particularly in the wake of major terrorist attacks, the reality is these are almost never unqualified. The near-universal revulsion against particular terrorist acts is not translated sufficiently into strategy and action against terrorists, or, crucially, into the acquisition of necessary and sufficient capacities to fight the scourge. Indeed, there is a powerful stream of *justification* that underlies the liberal democratic critique of terrorism, and it is this backdrop that gives terrorism its greatest force. *Terrorism works.* Given the moral ambivalence of the liberal-democratic world, its practitioners bear no permanent stigma and, under appropriate circumstances, are quickly able to re-invent themselves as advocates of 'peace', as political leaders, world statesmen, and even as worthy recipients of the Nobel Peace Prize—as was [Palestinian leader] Yasser Arafat. Across the world, and with strong manifestation in India, we see the most powerful advocacy—both by terrorist 'fellow travelers' and the ranks of 'good people' mouthing politically correct platitudes—of conciliation, appeasement and a range of inchoate political and developmental 'solutions', in the face of unending carnage. Indeed, after decades of unremitting terrorism in Jammu & Kashmir [a northern Indian state long torn by an insurgency and by territorial disputes with Pakistan] and the slaughter of tens of thousands of the very people the *jihadis* claimed to seek to 'liberate' (and the absolute denial of human and political rights to people in Pakistan occupied Kashmir, including the denial even of constitutional recognition to the people of Gilgit-Baltistan), Pakistan is able to rightly boast that it has been able to bring the 'Kashmir dispute' to the world's attention through its deceitful and bloody *jihad*.

Ideological Confusion

Contemporary terrorism draws enormous strength from two factors: the ample and predictable rewards it secures; and the legitimacy of extreme (terrorist) violence within particular societies, certainly those that benefit from this reward system, but also often including a number of societies that are directly threatened or targeted by such violence. Among those who claim adherence to the liberal democratic ideology, there is only an occasional voice that has seen fit to defend the constitutional order, and most have, willy-nilly, become apologists for those who engage in extreme and indiscriminate violence. With romanticised imagery and the strangest invention of arguments, even serious academicians arrive blindly at entirely preconceived conclusions, in [according to Michael Kinsley] an "astonishingly philistine, know-nothing posture, blocking any deeper understanding of the terrorist's mentality and motives". These justifications of terrorism, with little consistent evidence, continue to be advanced by those who proclaim and see themselves as advocates of freedom and nonviolence, and who argue that the response to such terrorism should not involve, or should minimise, use of force by the state. These arguments enjoy immense popularity, and they are constantly undermining the ability and capacity of democracies to effectively defend themselves against a pattern of warfare—often supported by inimical foreign powers—that constitutes an increasing threat to their very survival. . . .

Loss of Security

Decades of conceptual confusion and neglect have yielded a general and encompassing erosion—and in at least some extended regions, a collapse—of state capacities in the security sector, which have immensely encouraged disorders, extremism and violence. Cumulative infirmities in India's security sector have been immensely complicated by the continuous erosion of governance and administrative capacities; the degradation of grassroots politics and of cadre-based political organisation; the growth of inequalities and inequities, particularly in rural India; and a range of demographic factors, creating vast opportunities for extremist mobilisation. . . . The restoration of the authority and functions of governance, including development, health, education and basic social and human security, is consequently imperative and must constitute an integral part of any comprehensive approach to counterinsurgency and counterterrorism.

It must, nevertheless, be recognised that this can only be done after the restoration of a modicum of law and order, and hitherto unavailable efficiency in the operation of the justice system. The essential axiom, here, is that *you cannot develop what you do not control*—and dominance is, therefore, the first objective of any effective strategy to neutralise the onslaught of violent antistate movements.

The magnitude of the problem has now become so great that there is no possibility of dealing with it by mere tinkering or incremental augmentations and reforms—which appear to be the principal patterns of response at the national level, as well as in most states. The Group of Ministers' (GoM) report on national security, in February 2001, clearly noted that constitutional, legal and structural infirmities had "eroded the Union Government's authority to deal effectively with *any threat to the nation's security*", and called for "appropriate restructuring of the MHA [Ministry of Home Affairs]". Prime Minister Manmohan Singh has repeatedly emphasised the enormity of the crisis and, as far back as in June 2004, promised a "comprehensive approach" which would "create greater synergy between our intelligence agencies, closer coordination between internal security structures". Till the 26/11 attacks in Mumbai,[1] little of this had been translated into action. Post–26/11, there has been a flurry of activity. However, many of the most visible initiatives have, at best, been purely symbolic, while others have been no more than incremental. The combined impact of all such initiatives does not secure even a fraction of the critical mass that would be necessary to engineer an effective and efficient response to the terrorist and insurgent threats currently confronting the nation.

Poor Security Capacities

One of the major elements of the crisis is the country's extraordinarily poor capacities across the security spectrum. It is useful to look at some of the data in this regard:

Policing: There is a general policing deficit at all ranks, both in absolute numbers of sanctioned posts and in the numbers of vacancies that exist against such sanctioned posts.

Leadership: According to the Ministry of Home Affairs annual report for 2007–08, there is an over 16 per cent deficiency in numbers of IPS [Indian Police Service] officers in position as against sanctioned strengths.

This data may, indeed, understate the magnitude of the crisis in some crucial instances. Orissa, for instance, currently among the states facing an acute Maoist [Communist] challenge, has a total of 207 sanctioned posts in IPS ranks; there are presently just 84 officers in place. Sanctioned strength—

---

1. On November 26, 2008, Islamic terrorists detonated a number of bombs in Mumbai, killing 164 people.

approved years, if not decades ago—is deficient in most states, as against augmenting requirements.

Police Population Ratios (per 100,000 population): According to norms set by the United Nations, a minimum police to population ratio of 1:450 should be maintained for 'peacetime policing'. This works out to a ratio of 222 police personnel per 100,000 population. Most Western countries maintain ratios well above this minimum standard, and, for instance, the ratio is as high as 559 per 100,000 in Italy and 465 per 100,000 in Portugal. Significantly, most of these countries have policing needs that are certainly less demanding or extreme as compared to those confronting India, where the culture of the rule of law is far from entrenched and virtually all compliance needs enforcement. Yet, India's police to population ratio stands at a bare 125/100,000, and conditions in the states and areas most afflicted by disorders are often much worse.

For decades, proposals for police reforms have been kept in abeyance.

Police-Area Ratios: There is no standard norm for a minimal police-area ratio, and wide variations are possible here in view of demographic, geographical, political and administrative considerations. . . .

Some of the states worst afflicted by Maoist violence have the worst police-area ratios. Crucially, despite significant funding from the centre to the states underwriting police modernisation, security-related expenditures and augmentation of capacities, a substantial proportion of these funds are unspent or misspent each year.

Reforms Are Necessary

The challenges to policing cannot, however, be reduced to these quantitative indices alone. The quality of policing and the integrity of the institutional structures underlying police

Comparison of India's and Other Countries' Troop Strength

Country	Population	Active Duty Uniformed Troop Strength	Ratio of Population to Troops
India	1,147,995,904	1,325,000	866.41/1
Pakistan	172,800,048	620,000	278.71/1
UK	60,943,912	206,000	295.84/1
France	64,057,792	259,000	247.33/1
China	1,330,044,544	2,250,000	591.13/1
US	303,824,640	1,625,852	186.87/1

TAKEN FROM: Ajai Sahni, "National Responses to Terrorism," *Wars Within Borders: Occasional Writings on Sub-conventional Conflicts* (blog), South Asian Terrorism Portal, 2009. www.satp.org.

administration have long been an issue of contention. For decades, proposals for police reforms have been kept in abeyance, despite the urgent recommendations of numberless national and state police commissions, and notwithstanding the eventual intervention of the Supreme Court in September 2006, with a seven-point directive to immediately secure compliance on a small set of these recommendations. A comprehensive transformation of Indian police forces into a modern, democratic force would require the implementation of a wide range of these reforms as well as a comprehensive institutional *reinvention*, to equip them for contemporary and evolving challenges, including, particularly, terrorism, insurgency, and sub-conventional warfare, including emerging patterns sometimes described as 5th Generation Warfare.

Urgent containment initiatives also need to be launched in the immediate future, and the first stage of such a response relates to a more efficient mobilisation of existing capacities. Immediate steps can be taken to operationalise, retrain and reorient the maximum proportion of available police and intelligence resources, which are currently deployed on fairly wasteful patterns. Major initiatives are also possible to tap civilian resources and populations for surveillance, information generation and intelligence. The rapid acquisition and augmentation of technical and technological force multipliers can also help enhance the efficiency of responses in the near term.

The problem in India relates both to inadequate capacities to generate intelligence and to the utilisation and integration of a multiplicity of intelligence flows.

Military Capacities

India, rightly, takes great pride in its armed forces, boasting of the 'second largest army in the world'. At about 1.4 million, the current strength of the armed forces appears large in absolute terms. The reality, however, is that this strength is utterly inadequate in terms of the country's population, territory and strategic projections as an 'emerging global power'. India's ratio of active-duty uniformed troops to population works out to about 1:866. China's ratio is 1:591; UK [United Kingdom]—1:295; Pakistan—1:279; USA—1:187. Again, the Indian armed forces' technological and resource capabilities compare adversely to those of the modernised Western powers, and the army is way overstretched in conventional defence and counterinsurgency deployments. Critically, there is an acute and mounting crisis in leadership cadres. The army is short of 11,387 officers, against a current authorised strength of 46,615 (24.43 per cent deficit). The navy is 1,512 officers short of its sanction of 8,797 (deficit: 17.2 per cent). The air force needs 1,400 officers to meet its sanction of 12,128 (deficit: 11.5 per cent). During the last five years, 4,300 officers of the army, 1,177 officers of the air force and 1,096 officers of the navy have chosen to seek premature retirement or have resigned from the service. Despite a significant dilution of standards over the years, the armed forces are finding it impossible to recruit sufficiently even to maintain currently sanctioned strengths among officers.

As internal security crises multiply, this will become crucial. India's capacity to deal with emergent insurgencies and disorders, in the past, has relied on the reserve capacity of central paramilitary forces and the army, which allows a rapid redeployment of forces to tackle any abrupt crisis. However, with a continuous expansion of the theatres of violence and the consolidation of the 'protracted war' model of conflict, these reserve capacities are already under severe strain, and there is little residual 'surplus' now. The augmentation of permanent capacities to deal with any and all projected internal and external security threats is, consequently, an imperative, if the nation's future is to be secured in a planned and ordered trajectory.

Intelligence

The Kargil crisis [a 1999 war between India and Pakistan] had revealed glaring gaps in India's intelligence capacities and establishments and, nearly a decade later, the Mumbai 26/11 attacks demonstrated that little had been achieved in terms of addressing these. The problem in India relates both to inadequate capacities to generate intelligence and to the utilisation and integration of a multiplicity of intelligence flows. Even within a single-agency structure, the loss of operational intelligence in the complex network that exists between the field and the decision-making layers is enormous, and has often proven disastrous. The Kargil committee report had commented strongly on this 'loss' of field intelligence, and the calamitous impact it had on national security. The report called on India's intelligence establishment to take "an honest and in-depth stock of their present intelligence effort and capabilities to meet challenges and problems" and asked for a massive upgrading of technical, imaging, signal, electronic counterintelligence and economic intelligence capabilities, and a system-wide reform of conventional human-intelligence gathering.

Every suggestion in the report was accepted by the Group of Ministers, who released their recommendations in February 2001. Nevertheless, the recommendations of the report remained unimplemented, beyond a few symbolic changes, until 26/11, and cumulative deficits, backlogs and structural impediments have resulted in limited impact of sanctions approved thereafter. One of the recommendations called for a 'multiagency setup' to confront the challenges of terrorism, and this was, at least formally, implemented through the creation of two new wings under the IB: the Multi-Agency Centre (MAC) and the Joint Task Force on Intelligence (JTFI). MAC was charged with collecting and coordinating terrorism-related information from across the country; the JTFI is responsible for passing on this information to the state governments in real time. For years, both MAC and JTFI remained understaffed, under-equipped and ineffective, with even basic issues relating to their administration unsettled. Some of these issues have now received attention at the highest levels, but the principal objective, the creation of a national terrorism intelligence network and database, is yet far from realisation.

Israeli-Palestinian Peace Negotiations Must Not Be Derailed by Terrorist Attacks

Matthew Levitt

Matthew Levitt is a senior fellow and director of the Washington Institute for Near East Policy's Stein Program on Counterterrorism and Intelligence. In the following viewpoint, he argues that terrorist acts have often derailed the Palestinian peace process. He argues that for Israeli/Palestinian peace negotiations to be successful, both parties must be prepared to press on toward peace despite terrorist attacks or other crises. For this reason, he says discussing the possibility of terrorist attacks before they occur, along with putting plans in place to deal with them, is vital for the success of peace.

As you read, consider the following questions:

1. According to Levitt, when did the Oslo peace process collapse and what was the result?
2. How does Levitt define "pre-negotiations"?
3. How does Levitt say that the Israeli willingness to tolerate the lack of a Palestinian legal structure backfired?

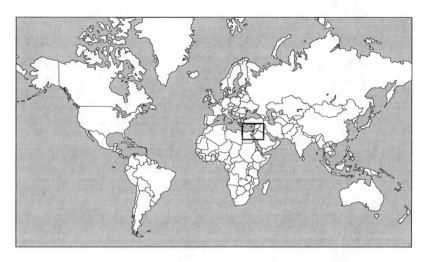

In calling for early elections, Mr. [Shimon] Peres is gambling that Israelis are satisfied with the relative success of the transfer of territory and political powers to the Palestinians, as with the reduction in terrorism. But all that could change with a new attack.

—Serge Schemann,
"Israeli Leader Launches Election Race,"
New York Times, *February 12, 1996*

4th Terror Blast in Israel Kills 14 at Mall in Tel Aviv; Nine-Day Toll Grows to 61; Peres Government Vows to Carry "War" into Palestinian Areas.

—Serge Schmemann,
"Bombing in Israel: The Overview;
4th Terror Blast in Israel Kills 14 at Mall
in Tel Aviv; Nine-Day Toll Grows to 61,"
New York Times, *March 5, 1996*

Oslo failed. Perhaps the [Palestinian-Israeli] peace process, inaugurated in Norway in 1993, was doomed from the outset, as some certainly argue. Both sides failed to meet their negotiation obligations, with Palestinian violence continuing to target Israelis, and Israeli settler activity continuing in the West Bank and Gaza Strip [Palestinian territory under Israeli control], throughout the peace process. When the parties did meet their obligations, they invariably did so behind schedule and in fits and starts. Among Israelis and their supporters, some concluded that Yasser Arafat [the Palestinian leader] and the Palestinian Authority never really intended to forswear violence and live in peace, side by side with Israel. Among Palestinians and their supporters, some concluded that Israel and its leaders never intended to end the occupation and enable the emergence of a sovereign Palestinian government. That may indeed have been the case for some decision makers on each side, but others clearly labored—in some cases at great personal expense—for the success of what by all accounts started out as an unexpected and historic breakthrough. Spoilers will always seek to undermine peace processes through acts of violence, but is there anything that can be done to insulate ongoing negotiations from the impact of these security crises and preserve peace talks in the face of terror acts? Of course, this assumes the parties truly are committed to pursuing peace and are ultimately willing to make sometimes painful concessions and then sell them at home to their constituencies. That may or may not be the case in any given peace process, including past and present efforts to secure and negotiate settlement to the Israeli-Palestinian conflict. As the international community tries to reinvigorate Israeli-Palestinian peacemaking, these questions are of critical importance. Despite its inherent flaws, and the fact that it ultimately did fail, was there anything that could have been done at the time to increase Oslo's odds of success?

Lessons from the Failed Peace

In September 2000, the peace process collapsed in the wake of that month's failed Camp David summit and ushered in six years of violence unprecedented even in the Israeli-Palestinian context. By January 2006, Palestinian politics was turned on its head as the militant Islamist group Hamas defeated the long dominant Fatah party in national elections and assumed majority control of the governing Palestinian Authority. For the vast majority of Israelis, the Hamas victory, coming just months after Israel's complete withdrawal from the Gaza Strip, underlined the already dominant position that unilateral moves like building a fence along the West Bank are the only answer to the perception that there are no credible Palestinian peace partners. This position was still further exacerbated after the Hamas takeover of Gaza in June 2007.

One of the key trends identified . . . is the importance of strengthening the status of policy legitimacy, negotiator authority, and credibility of the other party before being faced with a crisis.

How did the hopes for peace inaugurated with the 1993 Oslo peace process come to such a disastrous end? What lessons can be drawn from the failure of the Oslo peace process for future attempts to secure negotiated solutions to seemingly intractable ethnic, religious, and nationalist conflicts? What can be done to insulate ongoing negotiations from terror attacks and other acute security crises that will inevitably occur and threaten to undermine peace talks?. . .

The impact of acute security crises on ongoing negotiations represents one of the most significant facets of modern conflict resolution theory to remain under-researched. Ironically, it also stands out as the factor most likely to derail inherently sensitive negotiations. Events in Ireland, Sri Lanka, the former Yugoslavia, and the Middle East stand witness to the impact of targeted terror on ongoing negotiations over political reconciliation. These events unleash waves of public opposition to the very idea of sitting down to negotiate with those perceived as responsible for the crisis. How can decision makers cope with such incredible challenges? How are they to answer these challenges so that their constituents acknowledge their continued authority and legitimacy as negotiators? How can decision makers remain credible partners in the eyes of their negotiating partners in the wake of such events? How can decision makers sustain the legitimacy of a policy of continuing to negotiate in the face of barriers to conflict resolution erected by acute security crises? . . .

Preemptive Insulation

One of the key trends identified . . . is the importance of strengthening the status of policy legitimacy, negotiator authority, and credibility of the other party before being faced with a crisis. Equally important is the need to address security concerns on an ongoing basis so that when security crises do arise, their intensity is not compounded by coming on the heels of prior acts of violence. Preemptively addressing these issues would significantly reduce the potential intensity of future security crises, as well as the potency of their challenges to the factors of legitimacy.

The following recommendations are intended to serve as a model for the kind of proactive efforts needed to strengthen the negotiation process, bond both decision makers and their societies to that process, foster trust and a sense of partnership between the parties, and enhance the security of both parties through ongoing and cooperative efforts.

Pre-Negotiation

The term "pre-negotiation" usually refers to forging agreement on the parameters of a forthcoming negotiation process. Applied here, it would entail anticipating that crises will happen and negotiating in advance what types of actions would be taken in response to various types of crises. Part of the utility of negotiating or discussing these issues before a crisis happens is that post-crisis negotiations over concessions and face-saving gestures occur, by definition, under the stress of crisis conditions. Pre-negotiation discussions of these issues would

Government Responses to Terrorist Attacks

Hamas After Oslo

In the first few months after the signing of Oslo [peace accords in 1993], Hamas [a Palestinian radical Islamic organization] escalated attacks against Israeli soldiers and civilians alike. Attacks were carried out against civilian buses in Hadera and Afula (both in April 1994), Tel Aviv (October 1994), attacks against soldiers in Jerusalem (December 1994) and the Beit Lid junction (January 1995). In my conversation with him in Jerusalem October 2007, Israeli analyst Hillel Cohen described how individuals within Hamas, who he knew personally and who had hitherto opposed terrorist methods, gradually changed their minds about them. The shift in Hamas's tactics was precipitated by Baruch Goldstein's massacre of twenty-nine Palestinian worshippers at the cave of the patriarchs, in Hebron, in February 1994. Goldstein's actions were not seen as the work of an individual acting alone but rather as directed by Israeli agents. (In my visit to the cave, some thirteen odd years after the event, a local Palestinian 'guide' reinforced the point that this was not the isolated act of a disturbed individual; he hovered around me, constantly repeating the phrase 'Goldstein doctor, not crazy'). Hamas perpetrated an average of three terrorist attacks per year until the terrorist violence declined at the end of the 1990s.

Katerina Dalacoura,
Islamist Terrorism and Democracy in the Middle East.
New York: Cambridge University Press, 2011, p. 73.

provide a crisis-free baseline framework for post-crisis negotiations on crisis response and the terms for a resumption of talks. Many Israeli and Palestinian practitioners have come to this conclusion themselves, including a senior Palestinian intelligence official who stressed that "after attacks Israel usually comes with a unilateral response; there is a need for joint contingency plans."

While any decisions that were made would be informal and nonbinding, engaging in such an exercise would be extremely beneficial, if only because it would force the parties to acknowledge (to themselves, each other, and their societies) the likelihood that acute security crises will disrupt the peace process, and the need to find cooperative means of addressing that threat. It would also highlight the fact that the parties are sure both to suffer from legitimacy crises, and gain an opportunity and avenue for discussing means of boosting legitimacy in ways beneficial to both sides. Moreover, even if such pre-negotiation sessions produced no agreement on tactical measures for crisis response and management, they would further solidify the relationship between the parties and the sense of partnership between them and against extremist elements from both camps. At a strategic level, such partnership is no less important than agreement on tactical measures; indeed, strategic partnership is more often than not a necessary prerequisite for tactical cooperation.

The need for a strict adherence to the rule of law, for example, should not take second seat to the parties' efforts to provide a secure environment for negotiations.

Moreover, pre-negotiations could flush out other prerequisites for tactical success, such as how each party defines "peace" and what each party expects the peace process to look like. As an Israeli negotiator explained, the "majority of both sides want 'peace,' but see it differently." While the Israeli perception of peace stresses security and political normalization, Palestinians focus on independence, the ability to run their own affairs, and the prospect of a better quality of life. This Israeli official continued, the "peace process must move in [both] these directions or [you will] have a crisis." Similarly, pre-negotiations would provide an ideal setting for questioning one another's underlying assumptions in an effort to avoid the pitfalls of conducting negotiations under misplaced assumptions and presumed (and therefore unwritten) understandings.

Tangible issues could also be addressed in such pre-negotiation sessions. For example, the parties could come to terms on the need to deal with threats and tensions immediately and not let them simmer and grow over time. . . . Appropriate standing committees (with or without a third party) could be established to address small-scale issues as they present themselves and before they expand into larger-scale problems and act as crisis-multiplying factors by serving as a backdrop to future crises and exacerbating their perceived intensity.

Focusing on Long-Term Goals

Similarly, the parties could address the need not to sacrifice long-term objectives for short-term gains, as is frequently the case when it comes to security concerns in particular. The need for a strict adherence to the rule of law, for example, should not take second seat to the parties' efforts to provide a secure environment for negotiations. Indeed, the tendency to tolerate the lack of a comprehensive, formalized Palestinian legal structure (and the total disregard for what little legal structure there was), as long as Palestinians used that leeway to combat Palestinian extremists, would later backfire. Not only do such tactics breed more extremists, but the lack of a codified set of guidelines meant that security crackdowns were conducted if and when Palestinian decision makers were inclined to carry them out. At times, Palestinian leaders preferred trying to co-opt militants into the Palestinian Authority rather than arresting them, and even those arrested were subjected to a court system of the lowest judicial standards.

An additional benefit of such standing committees would simply come from having small groups of negotiators and substantive area experts organized in advance to contain the impact of a crisis on their given area of responsibility (such as joint patrols, incitement, prisoner releases, or settlement construction). An Israeli negotiator and security expert commented that a particularly successful tactic is to "require [a] small group [of negotiators] locked away for a period of time trying to work things out. Both sides [become] pretty practiced [and after a crisis the] hurt side can produce ideas or raise problems and questions." In such a setting, this official noted, suggestions can be aired openly and each side is better able "to understand the other side's situation, [work] together to work out a solution and then negotiate over wording and raising new issues." Especially useful in this regard would be a standing joint security committee that could meet periodically to outline prearranged modus operandi for crisis response. Having a guidebook offering a menu of possible responses to a variety of potential types of crises would be very useful, but it could never be—nor would it be intended to be—all inclusive. Unanticipated crises will surely arise, but having already worked together to bolster the negotiating process against outside challenges, and working off a template of various types of responses, the parties would be better placed to respond to the crisis cooperatively for the advance planning of their standing committee.

Periodical and Internet Sources Bibliography

The following articles have been selected to supplement the diverse views presented in this chapter.

BBC News — "Germany Tightens Airport Security over Attacks Threat," November 17, 2010. www.bbc.co.uk.

Daily News (New York) — "Peace Is Up to Palestinians: Unchecked Hamas Terrorists Could Derail Mideast Talks," September 4, 2010.

Uri Friedman — "Comparing How Norway and the U.S. Respond to Terror," *Atlantic*, July 27, 2011.

Glenn Greenwald — "An Un-American Response to the Oslo Attack," *Salon*, July 28, 2011. www.salon.com.

Nicholas Grono — "Australia's Response to Terrorism," Central Intelligence Agency, April 14, 2007. www.cia.gov.

Mark Magnier — "India's Response to Attacks Lays Bare Broader Failures," *Los Angeles Times*, December 1, 2008.

Tristana Moore — "Germany Heightens Security in Response to Terror Threat," *Time*, November 23, 2010.

Vladimir Solovyov — "Russia and NATO Prepare Joint Response to Terror," Russia Beyond the Headlines, March 14, 2011. http://rbth.ru.

Megan K. Stack — "Russia's Military Response to Muslim Militants Criticized in Wake of Moscow Subway Bombings," *Los Angeles Times*, March 30, 2010.

Jonathan S. Tobin — "The Proper Response to Terror," *Commentary*, March 14, 2011.

GLOBALVIEWPOINTS

CHAPTER 4

The Future of the War on Terror

In Afghanistan, the Death of Osama bin Laden Must Not End the War on Terror

Abbas Daiyar

Abbas Daiyar is a writer for Daily Outlook Afghanistan. *In the following viewpoint, he argues that Osama bin Laden's death is an important symbolic victory, but the threats of al Qaeda and the Taliban are not over. Rather, he argues, the United States should redouble the hunt for Taliban and al Qaeda leaders in Pakistan. He adds that Afghan leaders should not negotiate surrender to the Taliban, and American troops should not leave Afghanistan. Instead, he concludes, the death of bin Laden is a moment to press forward in the War on Terror.*

As you read, consider the following questions:

1. What did bin Laden tell his children in his will, according to Daiyar?
2. What differences does Daiyar see in the reaction to bin Laden's death in Pakistan and Afghanistan?
3. What does Daiyar say has strengthened his belief that talks with the Taliban are useless?

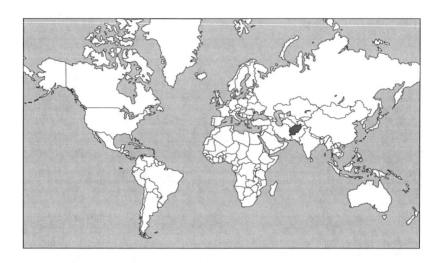

The man, who was responsible for mass murders of thousands of innocent people from America to Afghanistan, deserved that miserable death without a proper burial on earth. The leader of global terrorism who founded al Qaeda in his will written in December 2001 told his children not to join the group of bloodthirsty jihadis. This coward living in hiding for the last 10 years was an icon of inspiration for global terrorists, but for his own children, he didn't want the life he urged others to adopt. This should be the legacy of Osama bin Laden for all the radical Islamists who want to follow his path of bloodshed for political agenda.

Pakistani and Afghan Reaction

There were funeral prayers for bin Laden in Pakistani cities. I was horrified to watch one such prayer in Karachi where people were crying for him. Another homage rally was taken out in Quetta, the city where Taliban Shura[1] under Mullah Omar commands insurgency in the South. The homage rally

---

1. The Taliban is a radical Islamic group from Afghanistan. The Taliban controlled Afghanistan in the early 2000s and gave shelter to Osama bin Laden. A Shura is a consultation of leaders in Islamic tradition.

reminded me of a similar violent protest in Quetta in 2001 on the day when US air strikes were launched on the Taliban in Afghanistan. I was in Quetta in those days, and have seen the widespread public sympathy for bin Laden and the Taliban in that city. Religious political parties in Pakistan held rallies against the US raid and Osama's death on Friday after the noon prayers. While in Afghanistan, where bin Laden lived for years under the protection of his Taliban hosts, not a tear was shed. Rather, more than 10,000 Afghans in an anti-Taliban rally in Kabul on Thursday were saying "death to Osama". Street reaction in Afghanistan was joyful. No reaction was shown in Kandahar, the heartland of Taliban hosts of bin Laden or in the Tora Bora mountain region where Osama used to hide in caves.

It's very obvious that all the important leaders of the Afghan insurgency are hiding in Pakistani cities of Karachi and Quetta.

Of course the small funeral prayers and homage rallies in Pakistan do not represent majority public opinion in that nation. But those rallies were called by groups like Sipah-e-Sahaba—close to al Qaeda—and Jamaat-u-Dawa, the Kashmir[2]-oriented militant outfit whose chief is a most-wanted terrorist in India, but he was leading the Osama funeral prayers in Pakistan, without any action by security officials. The two-sided policy of Pakistan's security establishment towards militants has been under criticism by their media in a different tone than before, following the death of Osama in a compound next to Pakistan's military academy in Abbottabad, some kilometers away from the capital.

The reaction in Kabul [capital of Afghanistan] was, as expected, stirred with criticism of Pakistan. [Afghan] President

---

2. Kashmir is a long-disputed territory between India and Pakistan.

[Hamid] Karzai said the death of Osama in Abbottabad proved Kabul's stance that Osama was not in Afghanistan, and like many other al Qaeda and Taliban leaders, he was hiding across the border. Interior and defense ministers [General Abdul] Rahim Wardak and General Bismillah [Khan Mohammadi] told the Senate that Pakistan's intelligence agency ISI [Inter-Services Intelligence] was "keeping" the al Qaeda leader. They demanded the US Special Forces to target Mullah Omar and Gulbuddin Hekmatyar also, suggesting that the Taliban and Hezb-e-Islami [another radical Islamic group] leaders were also hiding in Pakistan.

Hiding in Pakistan

An Afghan intelligence official has claimed they helped the US pinpoint Osama's hideout. He said the Osama mansion was under surveillance since August [2010] last year. They thought a Taliban leader Maulavi Abdul Kabir was hiding there, and informed the US. Former NDS [National Directorate of Security] Chief Amrullah Saleh also said he had told Pervez Musharraf four years ago about Osama's presence around Abbottabad, but [the] former Pakistani president had smashed his fist on [the] table saying "Am I the President of the Republic of Banana?" Such stout was the denial from a general who is now surprised on Osama's hideout in Abbottabad.

The accusations of the Pakistan Army as an institution having links with al Qaeda or ISI being aware of Osama's presence in Abbottabad might not be true, otherwise the US should be more outspoken on this. But the fact that the most-wanted terrorist was hiding in their backyard for five years should make them hear concerns of Afghan officials, and not deny when the US intelligence officials say Taliban leaders are in Pakistan. It's very obvious that all the important leaders of the Afghan insurgency are hiding in Pakistani cities of Karachi and Quetta, while those of the Haqqani Network are operating from the safe havens of Waziristan [a region in northwest-

The United States Promises to Move Forward in the War on Terror

As President [Barack] Obama said last night, Usama bin Ladin is dead, and justice has been done. And today, I want to say a few words about what this means for our efforts going forward. . . .

In Afghanistan, we will continue taking the fight to al-Qaida and their Taliban allies, while working to support the Afghan people as they build a stronger government and begin to take responsibility for their own security. We are implementing the strategy for transition approved by NATO [North Atlantic Treat Organization] at the summit in Lisbon, and we [are] supporting an Afghan-led political process that seeks to isolate al-Qaida and end the insurgency. Our message to the Taliban remains the same, but today it may have even greater resonance: You cannot wait us out. You cannot defeat us. But you can make the choice to abandon al-Qaida and participate in a peaceful political process.

In Pakistan, we are committed to supporting the people and government as they defend their own democracy from violent extremism. Indeed, as the president said, bin Ladin had also declared war on Pakistan. He had ordered the killings of many innocent Pakistani men, women, and children. In recent years, the cooperation between our governments, militaries, and law enforcement agencies increased pressure on al-Qaida and the Taliban, and this progress must continue and we are committed to our partnership.

Hillary Rodham Clinton,
"Remarks on the Killing of Usama bin Ladin,"
US Department of State, May 2, 2011. www.state.gov.

ern Afghanistan, bordering Pakistan]. Pakistan knows about most of the Taliban leaders. The US has to further push the Pak military and intelligence establishment for an Osama-like manhunt of Taliban leaders.

Unfortunately in the US, the news of Osama's death has sparked calls for early withdrawal from Afghanistan. Afghans fear it very much.

Hunt for Other Leaders

The hunt of Osama should make Taliban and other insurgent leaders worried. President Karzai has sent his former Chief of Staff Omar Dawoodzai as ambassador to Pakistan and the purpose of this deployment is talks with the Taliban. Instead of a political surrender on the terms of insurgents, President Karzai should ask Pakistan to carry out military operations in North Waziristan and hunt down insurgent leaders. The US should conduct such special operations after Mullah Omar, Hekmatyar and the Haqqanis who are responsible for deaths of thousands of Americans, Afghans, and troops from other countries in Afghanistan, and countless innocent Afghan civilians.

The Pakistan military should now conduct operations in North Waziristan and Quetta, and arrest the Taliban leaders. Many senior leaders of al Qaeda are in Pakistan, and most probably the succession of Osama in replacing al Qaeda's leadership will also take place somewhere in tribal areas or any safe compound of a city, but the challenge for Pakistan is to stop it, and launch a manhunt of the remaining al Qaeda leadership. Only this way, the world will believe the presence of bin Laden in Abbottabad was a major intelligence failure, not any double-game.

Unfortunately in the US, the news of Osama's death has sparked calls for early withdrawal from Afghanistan. Afghans fear it very much, and it was this widespread concern that [American] Ambassador [to Afghanistan Karl] Eikenberry had to issue a statement saying "this victory will not mark the end of our effort against terrorism. America's strong support for the people of Afghanistan will continue as before." Death of Osama bin Laden is indeed the most important success of the war on terror. However, his demise won't make a big difference in this campaign as a blow to al Qaeda. He was a symbolic figure for the past many years, and there are far more radical masterminds to carry global terrorism as his successors.

Al Qaeda has confirmed the death of its founder and leader, threatening attacks on the US in retaliation. I am still skeptical of any success in the talks with the Taliban. My belief is further strengthened with the latest self-revelation by Maulvi Nazir, a Taliban commander in Waziristan, of his al Qaeda membership. In a recent interview to Saleem Shahzad of *Asia Times Online*, Maulvi Nazir has said the Taliban won't talk unless all foreign troops leave. "Al-Qaeda and the Taliban are one and the same. At an operational level we might have different strategies, but at the policy level we are one and the same," he said. Saleem Shahzad writes, "Nazir's affiliation with al-Qaeda seems to have passed unnoticed by the United States and NATO, which are investing heavily in a reconciliation process with the 'good Taliban' and they appear not to understand the drastic changes that have taken place among the top cadre of the Taliban."

Declare Victory and End the 'Global War on Terror'

Gideon Rachman

Gideon Rachman is the chief foreign affairs columnist for Finan-cial Times. *In the following viewpoint, Rachman argues that the death of Osama bin Laden is a good opportunity to end the War on Terror. He says that the government has wasted billions of dollars on the war. He argues that the threat of terrorism has been hyped and that concentrating on intelligence gathering distorts US foreign policy. He concludes that the next century will be shaped more by the rising economic powers in Asia than terrorist threats.*

As you read, consider the following questions:

1. What evidence does Rachman cite to back up his claim that the threat of terrorism has been hyped?
2. According to Rachman, how will the death of Osama bin Laden impact the US intelligence budget?
3. In Rachman's opinion, how will concentrating on intelligence gathering distort US foreign policy?

George W. Bush used to ask "why haven't we found bin Laden?" with such regularity that an exasperated official once suggested sending a one-sentence reply back to the president. "Because he's hiding."

Now, almost a decade after 9/11, Osama bin Laden has finally been found and killed. His death offers an opportunity to declare an end to the "war on terror." This is not the same as saying that the US and Europe can now stop worrying about terrorism. The West will need a serious counterterrorism policy for many years to come.

But the Bush-inspired drive to make terrorism the centrepiece of US foreign policy was a mistake. The declaration of a "Global War on Terror" distorted American foreign policy and led directly to two wars—in Iraq and Afghanistan. The war on terror has guzzled billions of dollars in wasteful spending and spawned a huge and secretive bureaucracy in Washington. The death of bin Laden gives President Barack Obama the cover he needs to start quietly unwinding some of these mistakes.

While good intelligence work is vital, there is plenty of evidence of massive waste and duplication in the US intelligence effort.

Getting the terrorist threat into perspective is difficult. The attacks on New York and Washington were so horrific that they are seared into the memory. It is also clear that al-Qaeda has spawned affiliates that may now be just as dangerous as the original al-Qaeda franchise, run by bin Laden from Pakistan. Intelligence officials say that dangerous plots are being hatched by branches of al-Qaeda in Yemen, Somalia and North Africa—and there is no reason to disbelieve them.

And yet, look at the numbers, and it becomes clear that the threat of terrorism has been seriously hyped. In a book published a couple of years ago John Mueller, a US academic, pointed out that the number of Americans killed by terrorists since 1960 is "about the same as the number killed over the same period by accident-causing deer." In a report for the RAND Corporation, Brian Jenkins made a similar point: "The average American has about a one in 9,000 chance of dying in

After the War on Terror

After the war on terror, American society will be better able to deny the remaining terrorists the ability to reach their primary goal: terror. The risk of attack will still exist, but if an attack takes place it will not provoke a dramatic foreign policy revolution or the restriction of the sorts of civil liberties that make America what it is and ought to be. As in other societies that have faced terrorism (the United Kingdom, Israel, India, and others), life will go on and people will go about their daily business without inordinate fear. The terrorists will see that the result of any attack was not the overreaction they sought to provoke but rather the stoic denial of their ability to provoke a counterproductive response.

Philip H. Gordon, Winning the Right War:
The Path to Security for America and the World.
New York: Times Books, 2007, p. 53.

an automobile accident and about a one in 18,000 chance of being murdered." However, in the five years after 9/11, and including the people killed there, "an average American had only a one in 500,000 chance of being killed in a terrorist attack."

Yet incredible resources have been poured into the "war on terror." In a report on "Top Secret America" published last year, the *Washington Post* pointed out that: "In Washington and the surrounding area, 33 building complexes for top-secret intelligence work are under construction or have been built since September 2001. Together they occupy the equivalent of almost three Pentagons." And that is just the organisations created since 9/11. The CIA and the National Security Agency were hardly modest or under-resourced organisations before the "war on terror."

By 2010, the US intelligence budget was $75 billion a year—a more than twentyfold increase since 9/11. That figure does not even include military activities run by the intelligence agencies, such as the drone attacks in Pakistan. Given all this, it is astonishing that it took a decade to track down bin Laden.

Nonetheless, the success in killing the leader of al-Qaeda—combined with warnings of new terrorist plots—may actually give a further boost to intelligence spending. This possibility is increased by the news announced last week that General David Petraeus, an empire-builder with a following on Capitol Hill, has been appointed as head of the CIA.

In fact, while good intelligence work is vital, there is plenty of evidence of massive waste and duplication in the US intelligence effort. According to the *Washington Post*, there are no fewer than 51 federal agencies entrusted with monitoring the flow of money to terrorist networks. The NSA intercepts 1.7 billion e-mails and phone calls every day—far more than could ever be usefully analysed.

An excessive concentration on intelligence-gathering is not just a waste of time and money. More important, it also distorts US foreign policy—as a dangerous merger takes place between intelligence and military capabilities. The line has already been blurred by the CIA's role in fighting the Afghan war. It will be further eroded by the appointment of a general to run the CIA. Meanwhile, as the spies and soldiers are showered with money, conventional diplomacy and development aid have been run on a relative shoestring.

Given the flow of resources, it is hardly surprising that US foreign policy has become so militarised over the past decade. And yet the results have been dismal. The war in Iraq cost hundreds of thousands of lives and probably made the terrorist threat worse. The utility of waging a decade-long war in Afghanistan also comes into question—now that we have confirmation that al-Qaeda's leadership was based deep inside Pakistan.

Meanwhile, as America poured money and resources into the GWOT, the truly epoch-making changes of our time were taking place in east Asia. The rise of new economic powers such as China and India—and the relative decline of the US—will ultimately shape the next century far more than the terrorist threat. But handling the rise of China and reviving the US economy are difficult and lengthy challenges—offering none of the emotional satisfaction of blowing away "America's most wanted."

VIEWPOINT 3

Pakistanis Fear
Economic Isolation

Daily Star

The Daily Star *is an English-language newspaper in Bangladesh. In the following viewpoint, it reports that Pakistanis are afraid of economic isolation due to their deteriorating relationship with the United States. The relationship between Pakistan and the United States began to deteriorate in 2011 after the discovery and death of Osama bin Laden in Pakistan. Pakistan fears that Washington might use its influence over financial institutions to harm the Pakistani economy.*

As you read, consider the following questions:

1. Who is Abdul Hafeez Sheikh?
2. According to the viewpoint, when did Pakistani-US relations begin to decline?
3. Sheikh believes it's not about US aid to Pakistan, but what that can pose a threat to Pakistan?

Pakistan's deteriorating relations with the United States may bring it international isolation on the economic front, Pakistan's finance minister Abdul Hafeez Sheikh yesterday [January 6, 2012] told the parliamentary committee tasked by the government to review bilateral terms with the US.

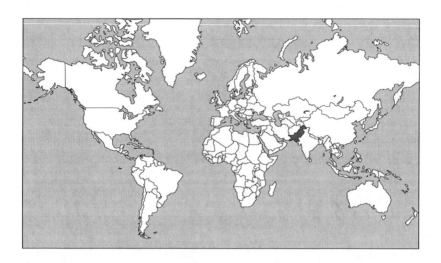

Pakistan-US Relations

Pakistan-US relations steadily declined in the beginning of 2011 after CIA [US Central Intelligence Agency] contractor Raymond Davis killed two Pakistani nationals in Lahore. This was followed by the US raid that killed Osama bin Laden in Abbottabad in May. The NATO-ISAF [North Atlantic Treaty Organization–International Security Assistance Force] incursion in November in the Mohmand tribal region which killed 24 Pakistani soldiers brought the ties to an all-time low with Islamabad [the capital of Pakistan] freezing the visa regime and transit facilities and the US freezing the military aid to Pakistan.

Sheikh warned that Washington might use its influence over international financial institutions to hurt the country's economic interests.

"There are some shocks Pakistan can absorb but there are others it can't," Abdul Hafeez Sheikh was quoted as telling members of the Parliamentary Committee on National Security (PCNS).

"A single incident must not determine our relations with the US," Sheikh said while referring to the steps taken by the government following the NATO aerial strikes. "Any decision should be taken while keeping in mind the multidimensional paradigm of security, prosperity of the country and economic diplomacy," he said.

Briefing the members of PCNS, Sheikh warned that Washington might use its influence over international financial institutions to hurt the country's economic interests.

"It is not about American aid but its clout over the IMF [International Monetary Fund], World Bank and other financial institutions that can pose a real challenge for us."

Shiekh briefed the 17-member committee in detail about the possible implications the country may face in the event of a move to pull out of the US alliance. The committee recently said that the basis of the new relationship should be conditional on the agreement to transfer civil nuclear technology to Pakistan.

The committee has finalised the draft recommendations and forwarded them to the defence and foreign ministries for their input. The government will then present the committee's proposals before a joint session of Parliament to seek its approval. The joint sitting is expected to be convened in mid-January.

The West Must Do More to End the Injustice That Motivates Jihad

Zia Haq

Zia Haq writes the blog They Call Me Muslim *for the Hindustan Times. In the following viewpoint, he argues that Osama bin Laden's death will not end global jihad. He says that terrorism thrives on the Islamic world's sense of injustice, which, he argues, is inflamed by Western policies. He says that bin Laden's ideology was opposed to Islam but that it has continuing appeal. He concludes that a just world order is needed to destroy the appeal of terrorism.*

As you read, consider the following questions:

1. What does Lawrence Wright say is at the bottom of Islamic extremism?
2. What groups does Haq list as branches of al Qaeda?
3. What conflicts does Haq list as needing resolution to end jihad?

[Terrorist group al Qaida's leader] Osama bin Laden's death [by American troops in May 2011] must be weighed against what conditioned—and continues to condition—global jihad. Or else, America's jubilation over the death of its Most Wanted may be short-lived.

Injustice and Jihad

The question everybody is asking now is: Are we done and is the world safe? 9/11 [September 11, 2001, terrorist attacks on the United States]—however traumatizing—was just one among many bloody manifestations of global jihad. But since it spectacularly struck at America's pride, a sense of national closure has come about with bin Laden's fall.

Arab states' own lack of capacity to give their citizens a sense of purpose and hope and unstable regimes fuelling nationalist jihadi insurgencies would all coalesce into a sweeping global form.

That thousands subscribed to one man's resolve of purging Western tutelage from Muslim lands ought not to be brushed aside, though Western policies cannot be considered to be the sole reason for jihadism [Islamic war]. Nonetheless, an unjust world order did serve as a necessary condition that shaped jihad in the 10 years before and after 9/11.

In *The Looming Tower[: Al-Qaeda and the Road to 9/11]*, the Pulitzer-winning biography of 9/11, Lawrence Wright sifts through Islamist extremism and finds at its bottom a "sense of deep humiliation".

Arab states' own lack of capacity to give their citizens a sense of purpose and hope and unstable regimes fuelling nationalist jihadi insurgencies would all coalesce into a sweeping global form.

Ultimately, Osama bin Laden was not dodging drones in mountain caves but passing days in bucolic retirement—much like an ageing business tycoon in his idyllic retreat. His empire was built, its core philosophy permanently etched, and its ranks staffed with ruthlessly efficient personnel.

Therefore, at the time he was taken down by US Navy SEALs, bin Laden was the chief mentor of a global enterprise that no longer required his hand-holding.

A look at global jihad's current structure should sober us down. [Bin] Laden's harvest had ripened into rich pickings: al Qaida in the Arabian Peninsula or AQAP, based in Yemen, al Qaida in Iraq or AQI, and al Qaida in the Islamic Maghreb or AQIM, based in North Africa.

Slaughtering of innocents, in itself, was never the goal, but it served as the means to achieve the goal of humbling the West. But because bin Laden failed to achieve any of his avowed goals, his means would become the end. The only thing to be achieved was the blood of innocents. That is why this was no jihad; nothing that could be validated even by bin Laden's own theological reasoning. If this was jihad, it was flawed to the very hilt.

Rather than shrink Western presence, bin Laden only provoked more interventions, including the ones in Iraq and Afghanistan. Pro-Western Islamic regimes, which [bin] Laden wanted to overthrow, would eventually be shaken not by his violent ideology, but by civilian uprisings. People would crave not for a caliphate but for democracy.

[Bin] Laden probably was aware that in his Holy War, there was no reasonable degree of success assured—a key historical requirement of jihad.

A just world order is not as difficult to achieve as is often thought. . . . It just needs global will, sincerity and honesty that international politics lacks.

Root Causes

However, bin Laden's death will do nothing to end the jihad he institutionalized. Global jihad's end will be made possible as much by a relentless pursuit of terrorism as by addressing its root causes.

Peace between Israel and Palestine, stability of Muslim countries, from Syria to Yemen, US withdrawal from Afghani-

---

Why Osama bin Laden Targeted the United States

[Osama bin Laden claimed] an anti-U.S. defensive jihad was mandatory for six reasons:

1. The U.S. military and civilian presence in the Prophet's homeland on the Arabian Peninsula

2. Washington's protection and support for tyrannical Muslim governments

3. Washington's unquestioning and unqualified support for Israel

4. Washington's support for countries that oppress Muslims, especially Russia, China, and India

5. U.S. and Western exploitation of Muslim energy resources at below-market prices

6. The U.S. military presence in the Muslim world outside the Arab Peninsula

Michael Scheuer, Osama bin Laden.
New York: Oxford University Press, 2011, pp. 112–113.

---

stan, tackling of Pakistan's duplicitous military and resolving the Kashmir issue [referring to a dispute over an area between India and Pakistan] are some tasks ahead. And many of these issues are tangled. Tackling Iran, for example, would require some positive development in Palestine.

The [United Nations] Security Council, in its statement on bin Laden's death, did touch upon this crucial aspect. Welcoming bin Laden's death, Ambassador Gérard Araud of France, which holds the rotating Security Council presidency, read out a presidential statement that said: "[t]hat terrorism will not be defeated by military force, law enforcement measures and intelligence operations alone, and can only be defeated by a sustained and comprehensive approach involving the active participation and collaboration of all States, and relevant international and regional organizations and civil society to address the conditions conducive to the spread of terrorism and to impede, impair, isolate and incapacitate the terrorist threat."

A just world order is not as difficult to achieve as is often thought. The mechanism already exists in the United Nations. It just needs global will, sincerity and honesty that international politics lacks.

To jihadis, the present world order will never make sense. Like it or not, a jihadi will never be able to understand why he is a "terrorist" while a head of state isn't—even if the latter's actions lead to civilians' deaths.

[Thomas] Hobbes [an English philosopher in the 1600s] was right to argue for public reason over private reason. The world, according to the Hobbesian legal framework, cannot function if everyone relies on "his own individualistic mode of reasoning", i.e., if everyone starts validating his judgement over others. If so, he warned in the *Leviathan*, life will be "nasty, brutish and short".

So, Hobbes said we must submit to a "sovereign authority". But [John] Locke famously argues against it, saying such an unconstrained authority would only create a "monster".

The underlying dynamics of jihad too are about one bloc's assertion of authority and another bloc's rejection of it (as the monster).

It will take a remedy of this situation before the world can dream of the last jihadi, much like bin Laden on his horse, fading away into the mountains.

The Muslim World Must Do More to Reject Jihad

Abdullah Iskandar

Abdullah Iskandar is a writer for the pan-Arab newspaper Dar Al Hayat. *In the following viewpoint, he argues that Osama bin Laden's death may not end terrorist actions by al Qaeda. However, he says that the most dangerous legacy of bin Laden may be the way that some in the Arab world have apologized for his actions. Iskandar says some commentators have argued that bin Laden was merely misguided and that he was correct that violence is justified to fight against injustice. Iskandar rejects this argument and says that Muslims need to condemn bin Laden's violence consistently and must not glorify his memory.*

As you read, consider the following questions:

1. Why does Iskandar say it was not a coincidence that al Qaeda was linked to organized crime?
2. According to Iskandar, what do many commentators feel was bin Laden's "mistake"?
3. What words do some of those who do not condemn bin Laden use to describe him, according to Iskandar?

Expressions such as a new turn and the end of a stage in the war on terrorism are being used by the majority of the comments over the liquidation of [terrorist group Al-Qaeda

Abdullah Iskandar, "Is This the End of Terrorism?," *Dar Al Hayat*, May 4, 2011. All rights reserved. Reprinted by permission.

leader] Osama bin Laden at the hands of the American troops in Pakistan [in May 2011]. This is based on the assumption that bin Laden is standing at the head of a central and hierarchal organization that has as many branches around the world as there are armed groups proclaiming their affiliation with Al-Qaeda. In order for bin Laden's death to constitute a turn and the end of a stage, one must also assume that the man was planning and issuing orders that were being respected at the level of all the terrorist operations around the world, especially after his disappearance following the ousting of the regime of his allies—the Taliban [a militant Afghan Islamic group]—from the authority in Afghanistan.

Al-Qaeda Is Not Dead

However, the belief of such assumptions would in turn require a certain level of naïveté. Indeed, ever since his alliance with Ayman al-Zawahiri [another Al-Qaeda leader] to form their front against the Christians and the Jews [in 1998], the man's name was linked to terrorist operations. However, the situation changed drastically after they both fled under the pressures of the American war machine in Afghanistan [in 2001, when the United States invaded Afghanistan] and after it became very difficult for them to supervise terrorist operations, not because of their abstinence, but for purely logistic reasons.

> *The most dangerous thing we heard . . . was the defense of the criminal acts committed by bin Laden before he disappeared in Afghanistan.*

Still, such resounding operations continued to occur despite the two men's hiding, at the hands of armed groups drawing inspiration from the theories of Al-Qaeda and justifying their terrorism by their loyalty to this organization. This means that the latter terrorists were not awaiting the planning or central orders of bin Laden and his deputy to kidnap, kill or detonate. One can even say that outlaw gangs intentionally proclaimed their loyalty to the organization to justify their acts in many areas around the world, while it is not a coincidence—in that sense—that the names of numerous people who proclaimed their loyalty to Al-Qaeda were linked to organized crime.

No Defense for Al-Qaeda

At this level, a lot should be done in the face of these gangs in many areas of the world, before concluding that the defeat has affected bin Laden's organization and that the war on the latter has entered a new turn.

But the most dangerous thing we heard—especially coming from commentators and politicians belonging to political Islam—was the defense of the criminal acts committed by bin Laden before he disappeared in Afghanistan.

Indeed, the latter comments focused on two points, the first being the fact that the man "worked hard but may have committed a mistake," and the second linking his "mistake" to oppressive practices to which the Muslims were subjected at the hands of the West.

In other words, these positions summoned up the roots of bin Laden's theory which considers that diligence resides in violence and its different manifestations, and that the mistake resides in the targeting of the Muslims, and is justified as long as there is oppression practiced against Muslims. However, the concept of this injustice is vague and cannot be defined. In the opinion of the latter, it extends over all the territories where Muslims are present, and not just the injustice affecting the people of Palestine at the hands of Israel and its protector the United States, knowing that the terrorism of Al-Qaeda hit all the locations except Palestine.

This actually means that violence as a political tool is not condemned in itself, and that the condemnation rather affects its "divergence" away from its real battle which is to be defined based on the political circumstances. Therefore, some of the latter did not hesitate to describe bin Laden as being a "mujahid" [Islamic fighter] and a "martyr," thus acquitting him from all the terrorist acts for which he bluntly proclaimed his responsibility and from all his public calls for killing and liquidation. These positions thus restore the status of the prodigal son who relinquished his organizational roots to form his own group.

Today, with the eruption of the Arab protests [referring to the Arab Spring democracy movement across the Middle East that began in December 2010] through which political Islam is regaining some of its momentum while benefitting from the popular demands to plurality and democracy, these positions toward "what is wrong" and violence constitute a major challenge, without bin Laden—whether alive or dead—having any impact on its confrontation.

In the West, Osama bin Laden's Death Should Not Be an Excuse for Racism or Hate

Ray Hanania

Ray Hanania is an Arab American, Palestinian Christian jour-nalist. In the following viewpoint, he says that Osama bin Laden's death provoked celebrations of violence and anti-Muslim rhetoric in the West. He says the reaction shows the lack of edu-cation in the West about Arabs and Islam. He adds that this has resulted in flawed American policy in Afghanistan and Iraq. He concludes that the West must not demonize Islam but should in-stead strive for peace and understanding.

As you read, consider the following questions:

1. What does Hanania object to on the "Bin Laden is Dead" Facebook page?
2. Where does Hanania say he was on the day that Terry Jones was taunting Arab Muslims?
3. What does Hanania say is the proper way to respond to conflict or violence?

As America celebrates the death of our number one enemy, Osama bin Laden [head of the terrorist group Al-Qaida], we should remind ourselves that we are not like the terrorists.

Racist Hatred

That means we shouldn't act like they do. Bin Laden claimed he attacked America to achieve justice for the Muslim world, though he was never a spokesman for that world.

Too many Americans on Facebook, Twitter and other social media sites are using the bin Laden killing as an excuse to vent their racist hatred of Muslims and Arabs.

Instead of showing how much better we are than the enemy, some people are showing that they are not much different.

On several major sites, such as the "Bin Laden is Dead" Facebook page, too many "celebrants" expressed their glee with words like, "Go back to riding your camels and wearing that dot on your head." (Dots on foreheads are not Arab or Muslim, of course, but an angry racist would not be educated enough to know that.)

There are worse comments calling for the killing of all Muslims and Arabs on many Facebook pages.

Instead of showing how much better we are than the enemy, some people are showing that they are not much different. Bin Laden's hatred was racist and vicious. We saw a similar hatred in Terry Jones, the pastor from Gainesville, Florida, who burned copies of the Koran, provoking a massacre of UN [United Nations] staff in Afghanistan last month [February 2011].

Yet while Terry Jones received wide coverage in general, the great things American Arabs and Muslims do in this country go largely unnoticed. The mainstream media sometimes ignore the racist foundations of such celebrations.

For example, the very day that a horde of media was covering Terry Jones's taunting Arab Muslims in Dearborn, I was down the street there presiding over the 18th Annual Dinner of Life for Relief, one of the nation's most reputable charitable organizations, detailing all that has been done to support Muslim orphans and those in need across the world with no media coverage, of course.

Americans are largely uneducated about the Middle East. They know little about the Arab world, the Islamic world or the Middle East, yet that lack of knowledge has become the foundation of our American foreign policy. It took us almost 10 years to kill bin Laden. Former president George W. Bush failed after starting wars in Afghanistan and Iraq.

We're stuck in the ongoing war in Afghanistan. A war we are not winning. Bin Laden's death is not going to change things on that front. We are stuck in a war in Iraq—one we should never have started, but which we can't leave either.

None of these actions has made America safer; they have only delayed the violence that will surely follow.

More Education Is Needed

The pro-democracy revolutions in the Middle East where citizens are rising in opposition to dictatorships [in countries like Egypt and Syria] is a stark contrast to the message that bin Laden tried to make with Al-Qaida killing innocent civilians. Change can come through protests and demonstrations when they are founded in moral principle, but change driven by violence and terrorism always ends in violence and failure for the terrorists.

Western nations that are most concerned about Middle Eastern violence should spend more resources on supporting the citizens of the Arab world rather than supporting their dictators and then finding they need to use military violence to bring some of them down.

America could be a stronger and better country if instead of celebrating a military victory with hateful and racist chants against Muslims and Arabs in America—Muslims and Arabs who have served proudly and patriotically in the US military—we tried to educate our children so they can understand how to confront the challenges we face more successfully.

Western nations could start trying to teach their citizens how to understand the true face of Islam, for example, or the political dynamics of the Middle East conflict rather than allowing a media frenzy to lead the people into embracing racist stereotypes of Arabs and Muslims or believing the political spin.

We must respect all life. We should never celebrate anyone's death.

When it takes 10 years to bring a murderer like bin Laden to justice, it says something about our failures in foreign policy and our lack of knowledge about the regions we fear. Some people around the world view America the same way Americans view Al-Qaida, the terrorist organization bin Laden founded. They see us as the terrorists when we strike out at Libya's Muammar Gaddafi and kill his son and grandchildren [through missile strikes in May 2011].

Are we only protecting ourselves, while claiming to be the leaders of the free world?

It was a mistake to bury bin Laden's body at sea without first providing absolute visual verification of his death. Photographs will not be enough. His life will become a standard for millions of others who will try to attack us the way he did, unless we can change how we view others.

We must respect all life. We should never celebrate anyone's death. We should champion civil rights and respond to terrorism, not like terrorists, but rather as the highly civilized people we insist we are.

The proper way to respond to conflict is education and understanding. Israelis and Palestinians would be wise to embrace that strategy for peace. And the proper way to respond to violence is to step up the activism for peace and education about the people we fear or, simply, really do not understand.

Periodical and Internet Sources Bibliography

The following articles have been selected to supplement the diverse views presented in this chapter.

Peter Bergen	"The Terrorists Among Us," *Foreign Policy*, November 19, 2009.
Economist	"After Osama bin Laden: They Got Him," May 5, 2011.
Earl Ofari Hutchinson	"Bin Laden Death Brings Resurgence of Anti-Muslim Racism," TheGrio.com, May 5, 2011. www.thegrio.com.
Mark N. Katz	"The 'War on Terror': Future Directions," Middle East Policy Council, January 25, 2011. www.mepc.org.
Masood-Ur-Rehman Khattak	"Pakistan's Sovereignty and Future of War Against Terror," Eurasia Review, May 13, 2011. www.eurasiareview.com.
Stuart Levey, as told to Tess Vigeland	"What bin Laden's Death Means for Future Financing Against Terrorism," Marketplace, May 2, 2011. www.marketplace.org.
Dahlia Lithwick	"Closing Pandora's Box," *Slate*, May 2, 2011. www.slate.com.
Moshe Phillips	"Beinart's Wrong Again—The War on Terror Is Not Over," *American Thinker*, May 7, 2011.
Walter Rodgers	"Osama bin Laden: A Fraud and a Failure," *Christian Science Monitor*, May 5, 2011.
Room for Debate (blog)	"The War on Terror After Osama bin Laden," May 2, 2011. www.nytimes.com.
Charlie Szrom	"Considering the Future of the War on Terror," *Weekly Standard*, May 2, 2011.

For Further Discussion

Chapter 1

1. One argument for America's continued involvement in Afghanistan is that if the United States does not continue to commit troops to the country, Afghanistan will become a failed state and a breeding ground for terrorism. Based on the viewpoints by Max Boot and Paul D. Williams, is this a convincing argument for US involvement in Afghanistan? Explain your reasoning.

2. Research the Oslo, Norway, terrorist attacks of 2011. Can these attacks be explained by poverty, inequality, Islam, or failed states? Do any explanations in this chapter help to explain what caused the Norway terrorist attacks?

Chapter 2

1. Based on the viewpoints in this chapter, in what ways might preserving human rights *help* in the War on Terror?

2. Based on the readings in this chapter, do you believe there is ever a time when human rights might be violated in order to combat terrorism? Explain your answer.

Chapter 3

1. Based on the *Spiegel* viewpoint, would you be willing to undergo a search by a full-body scanner in an airport for security purposes? Explain your reasoning.

2. As the viewpoint by Ajai Sahni suggests, India's problem with terrorism has been caused in part by its tense relationship with its neighbor Pakistan. Based on Matthew Levitt's viewpoint, what problems might India and Paki-

stan face from terrorism if they attempted to hold peace talks? How does Levitt suggest they might confront these problems?

Chapter 4

1. Based on the viewpoints in this chapter, did Osama bin Laden's death change the War on Terror in important ways? Explain your answer.

2. Based on the viewpoints in this chapter, what would need to happen for the United States to declare the War on Terror over? Should the United States ever end the War on Terror? Explain your answers.

Organizations to Contact

The editors have compiled the following list of organizations concerned with the issues debated in this book. The descriptions are derived from materials provided by the organizations. All have publications or information available for interested readers. The list was compiled on the date of publication of the present volume; the information provided here may change. Be aware that many organizations take several weeks or longer to respond to inquiries, so allow as much time as possible.

Begin-Sadat Center for Strategic Studies (BESA)
Bar-Ilan University, Ramat Gan   52900
   Israel
972-3-535-9198 • fax: 972-3-535-9195
e-mail: besa.center@mail.biu.ac.il
website: www.biu.ac.il/Besa/

The Begin-Sadat Center for Strategic Studies (BESA) seeks to contribute to the advancement of Middle East peace and security, especially as it relates to the national security and foreign policy of Israel, by conducting policy-relevant research on strategic subjects. It publishes monographs and periodical series, as well as frequent papers and a biannual news bulletin. Papers and bulletins are available through its website.

Brookings Institution
1775 Massachusetts Avenue NW, Washington, DC   20036
(202) 797-6000
e-mail: communications@brookings.edu
website: www.brookings.edu

The Brookings Institution, founded in 1927, is a liberal think tank that conducts research and education in foreign policy, economics, government, and the social sciences. It publishes numerous books and the quarterly *Brookings Review*. Its website includes numerous papers and articles, including "The Taliban and Air Control in Afghanistan" and "Norway's Oklahoma City?"

Cato Institute

1000 Massachusetts Avenue NW
Washington, DC   20001-5403
(202) 842-0200 • fax: (202) 842-3490
website: www.cato.org

The Cato Institute is a libertarian public policy research foundation dedicated to increasing the understanding of public policies based on the principles of limited government, free markets, individual liberty, and peace. It publishes the tri-annual *Cato Journal*; the periodic *Cato Policy Analysis*; and a bimonthly newsletter, *Cato Policy Review*. Its website includes articles such as "Pakistan, Afghanistan, and Terrorism" and "A Not-So-Global War on Terrorism."

Council on Foreign Relations

58 E. Sixty-Eighth Street, New York, NY   10065
(212) 434-9400 • fax: (212) 434-9800
e-mail: communications@cfr.org
website: www.cfr.org

The Council on Foreign Relations researches the international aspects of American economic and political policies. Its journal *Foreign Affairs*, published five times a year, provides analysis on global conflicts. Articles on its website include "Terrorism Concerns After bin Laden" and "Terrorism Trials and Detention's Future."

Human Rights Watch (HRW)

350 Fifth Avenue, 34th Floor, New York, NY   10118-3299
(212) 290-4700 • fax: (212) 736-1300
e-mail: hrwnyc@hrw.org
website: www.hrw.org

Human Rights Watch (HRW) is an international organization dedicated to ensuring that the human rights of individuals worldwide are observed and protected. To achieve this protection, HRW investigates allegations of human rights abuses then works to hold violators, be it governments or individuals, accountable for their actions. The organization's website is divided by continent, offering specific information on individual countries and issues. Articles on terrorism include "Fighting Terrorism Fairly and Effectively" and "In the Name of Counter-Terrorism: Human Rights Abuses Worldwide."

Institute for Afghan Studies (IAS)

e-mail: info@institute-for-afghan-studies.org
website: www.institute-for-afghan-studies.org

Funded and run by young Afghan scholars from around the world, the Institute for Afghan Studies (IAS) seeks to promote a better understanding of Afghanistan through scholarly research and studies. The IAS website provides a wealth of information on the history and politics of Afghanistan, including weekly political analyses, reports and articles, and biographical information on key figures in Afghanistan's politics.

Institute of Southeast Asian Studies (ISEAS)

30 Heng Mui Keng Terrace, Pasir Panjang   119614
   Singapore
(65) 6778 0955 • fax: (65) 6778 1735
e-mail: admin@iseas.edu.org
website: www.iseas.edu.sg

The Institute of Southeast Asian Studies (ISEAS) is a regional research center dedicated to the study of sociopolitical, security, and economic trends and developments in Southeast Asia. It conducts research programs, holds conferences, and provides a range of research support facilities. It is home to ISEAS Publications, which has produced important scholarly books on piracy in Indonesia and the Malacca Strait. It also publishes journals, annuals, and a newsletter. Articles on terrorism include "Osama's Death Will Not End Terrorist Attacks" and "Attacks May Be to Yingluck's Advantage."

Muslim Council of Britain (MCB)

PO Box 57330, London El 2WJ
+44 (0) 845 26 26 786 • fax: +44 (0) 207 247 7079
e-mail: admin@mcb.org.uk
website: www.mcb.org.uk/index.php

The Muslim Council of Britain (MCB) is a national British representative Muslim umbrella body with more than five hundred affiliated national, regional, and local organizations, mosques, charities, and schools. It works to promote a just position for Muslims within British society. Its website includes many articles on the War on Terror, including "MCB Welcomes Prime Minister's Strategy to Tackle Terrorism."

RAND Corporation

1776 Main Street, PO Box 2138
Santa Monica, CA   90407-2138
(310) 393-0411 • fax: (310) 393-4818
website: www.rand.org

The RAND Corporation is a nonprofit institution that helps improve policy and decision making through research and analysis. The corporation has studied terrorism for more than thirty years and has published numerous books on that subject as well as foreign policy and national security. Research papers on these topics are also available on the RAND website.

US Department of Homeland Security (DHS)

Washington, DC   20528
(202) 282-8000
website: www.dhs.gov/index.shtm

Created just after the September 11, 2001, terrorist attacks on the United States, the Department of Homeland Security (DHS) was envisioned as a central agency that could coordinate federal, state, and local resources to prevent or respond to threats to the American homeland. The DHS contains many subdivisions that deal specifically with trade, immigration, preparedness, and research. The DHS website contains mission statements and department performance records, as well as speeches and congressional testimony by DHS representatives.

Bibliography of Books

A. Alan Borovoy   *Categorically Incorrect: Ethical Fallacies in Canada's War on Terrorism.* Toronto, Ontario: Dundurn, 2006.

Daniel Byman   *Deadly Connections: States That Sponsor Terrorism.* New York: Cambridge University Press, 2007.

Avner Cohen   *Worst-Kept Secret: Israel's Bargain with the Bomb.* New York: Columbia University Press, 2010.

Tracy Dahlby   *Allah's Torch: A Report from Behind the Scenes in Asia's War on Terror.* New York: William Morrow, 2005.

R. Hrair Dekmejian   *Spectrum of Terror.* Washington, DC: CQ Press, 2007.

Emma Gilligan   *Terror in Chechnya: Russia and the Tragedy of Civilians in War.* Princeton, NJ: Princeton University Press, 2010.

Minton F. Goldman   *Rivalry in Eurasia: Russia, the United States, and the War on Terror.* Westport, CT: Praeger, 2009.

Rohan Gunaratna and Khuram Iqbal   *Pakistan: Terrorism Ground Zero.* London, UK: Reaktion Books, 2011.

Steve Hewitt   *The British War on Terror: Terrorism and Counter-Terrorism on the Home Front Since 9/11.* New York: Continuum Books, 2008.

Bruce Hoffman   *Inside Terrorism*. New York: Columbia University Press, 2006.

Tikva Honig-Parnass and Toufic Haddad, eds.   *Between the Lines: Readings on Israel, the Palestinians and the U.S. "War on Terror."* Chicago, IL: Haymarket Books, 2007.

Zubeda Jalalzai and David Jefferess, eds.   *Globalizing Afghanistan: Terrorism, War, and the Rhetoric of Nation Building.* Durham, NC: Duke University Press, 2011.

Steven Kettell   *New Labour and the New World Order: Britain's Role in the War on Terror.* Manchester, UK: Manchester University Press, 2011.

Mahmood Mamdani   *Good Muslim, Bad Muslim: America, the Cold War, and the Roots of Terror.* Johannesburg, South Africa: Jacana Media, 2005.

Steve Marsh and Wyn Rees   *The European Union in the Security of Europe: From Cold War to Terror War.* New York: Routledge, 2012.

Jane Mayer   *The Dark Side: The Inside Story of How the War on Terror Turned into a War on American Ideals.* New York: Anchor Books, 2009.

Ken Menkhaus   *Somalia: State Collapse and the Threat of Terrorism.* New York: Oxford University Press, 2004.

Giulio Meotti   *A New Shoah: The Untold Story of Israel's Victims of Terrorism.* New York: Encounter Books, 2010.

Robert G. Rabil *Syria, the United States, and the War on Terror in the Middle East.* Westport, CT: Praeger, 2006.

John Russell *Chechnya—Russia's 'War on Terror.'* New York: Routledge, 2007.

Syed Saleem Shahzad *Inside Al-Qaeda and the Taliban: Beyond Bin Laden and 9/11.* New York: Pluto Press, 2011.

Bilveer Singh *The Talibanization of Southeast Asia: Losing the War on Terror to Islamist Extremists.* Westport, CT: Praeger, 2007.

Ujjwal Kumar Singh *The State, Democracy and Anti-Terror Laws in India.* Thousand Oaks, CA: Sage Publications, 2007.

Peter Tomsen *The Wars of Afghanistan: Messianic Terrorism, Tribal Conflicts, and the Failures of Great Powers.* New York: PublicAffairs, 2011.

Martin I. Wayne *China's War on Terrorism: Counter-Insurgency, Politics, and Internal Security.* New York: Routledge, 2008.

Index

Geographic headings and page numbers in **boldface** refer to viewpoints about that country or region.

A

A. v. UK (1998), 60

Abdulmutallab, Umar Farouk, 106, 107, 108, 112

Abu Ghraib prison, Iraq, 75

Abu Hamza, 70

Afghanistan, 89–93, 141–147

  death of bin Laden must not end the war on terror, 141–147

  improving women's rights aids war on terror, 89–93

  independence, 145

  al-Qaeda history, 31, 32, 142–143, 144, 163

  radicalization, 118

  Russian war, 104

  should not negotiate with Taliban, 141, 145, 146

  terrorist training, 70

  UN members killed, 167

Afghanistan conflict, 2001–

  American errors, 149, 151, 168

  American troops still needed, 141, 146–147

  American withdrawal, 159–160

  Australian troops and involvement, 14, 16–17

  insurgency members in Pakistan, 144, 146

  NATO involvement, 25, 28, 145

  terrorism within, 25, 163

  terrorist recruiting, 90

Africa

  al-Qaeda in, 149

  US foreign and national security policy, 34

  See also specific nations

Air Transportation Safety Act (US; 2002), 71–72

Airport body scanners, 106–112

Al Itihad Al Islamiya (militant Islamic group), 35

al Sadr, Muqata, 41

al-Masri, Abu Hamza, 70

al-Qaeda. *See under* Q

al-Qaradawi, Sheikh Yusuf, 70

al-Zawahiri, Ayman, 163

"Amrozi," 87

Anti-Terrorism, Crime and Security Act (United Kingdom; 2001), 56–58, 60, 63

Anti-terrorism efforts. *See* Counterterrorism

Apologism, for terrorism, 120, 121–122, 162, 164–165

Arab nationalism, 39, 40

Arab Spring movement, 165, 168

Arab-Israeli conflict, 40, 42, 130–138, 159, 160

Arafat, Yasser, 41, 42, 121, 132

Arafat, Yasir. *See* Arafat, Yasser

Araud, Gérard, 160–161

Argentina, 49

Asian economic power, 148, 152

Australia, 14–17

B

Ba'ashir, Abu Bakar, 87
Bakri Mohammad, Omar, 70
Bali, Indonesia terrorism attacks (October, 2002), 15, 87
Bandits, 38
Bandt, Adam, 16–17
Bangladesh, 116, 118
Barcham, Manuhuia, 33
Barroso, José Manuel, 76
bin Laden, Osama
    death, 141–147, 148, 149, 151, 154, 157, 158, 166–170, 169
    hunt for, 76, 99, 144, 148–149, 151, 169
    leadership/influence, 32, 42, 142, 157, 158–159, 160, 162–165, 167
    tribal conflict, 39, 41
bin Nurhasyim, Amrozi, 87
Bingham, Lord, 57
Blair, Tony, 98–99
Blanchett, Cate, 15
Body scanners, 106–112
Boot, Max, 24–29
Borders, geographic
    India, 116–117, 121–122
    West Bank (fence), 133
Bosnia, 27
Brazilian Muslim communities, 44, 47, 48, 49, 50
Breivik, Anders Behring, 97, 99
Britain. See United Kingdom
British imperialism, 27
British nationals, 57
Brown, Lord, 59, 61–62
Bukovac, Matthew, 27
Bush, George W., and administration
    bin Laden hunt, 148
    rendition policies, 75
    September 11 terrorist attacks, 99
    tax cuts, 22–23
    war on terror, and wars, 149, 168

C

Camp David peace summit, 2000, 132
Casualties, totals, 14, 15, 149–150
Caucasus-Moscow relations, 103–104
Central Intelligence Agency (CIA), 67, 75, 76, 150, 151, 154
Chahal v. United Kingdom (1996), 55
Charter of Fundamental Rights (EU), 71
China, 78–83
    economy, 82–83, 148, 152
    Tibet policy, 81, 83
    uses war on terror to repress Uighur separatist movements, 78–83
Chinese Communist Party, 81, 82
Christian fundamentalist terrorism, 96, 97, 99
Christianity tenets, 40
Chung, Chien-peng, 78–83
Clarke, Charles, 62–63, 98
Clinton, Hillary Rodham, 145
Cohen, Hillel, 135
Communism, 33, 81, 82
Control order cases, 59–62, 71
Convention for the Protection of Human Rights and Fundamental Freedoms (Europe), 54–55, 64, 71
Costs of war on terror, 148, 150–151
Council of Europe, 54–55, 71

Counterterrorism
  Australia, 14–17
  China, 78–83
  eradicating injustice, 157–161
  Europe, 66, 67, 68–77, 149
  Germany, 107, 109–110, 112
  India, 113–119, 120–129
  Norway, 100–101
  Pakistan, 91–93
  rejecting jihad, 162–165
  Russia, 102, 104–105
  United Kingdom, 56–62, 63,
    68–69, 71, 98–99
  United States, 66, 67, 68, 71–
    77, 84–88, 99, 148, 149, 150–
    151
Courts
  control order cases, 59–62
  European Court of Human
    Rights, 55, 60, 62
  human rights protection, 53,
    54–56, 57, 58–59
  Special Immigration Appeals
    Commission (UK), 59–61
Cronin, A.K., 32
Cuba, 45
Cults of personality, 42
Curfews, 58–59, 71

D

The Daily Star, 153–156
Daiyar, Abbas, 141–147
Dalacoura, Katerina, 135
Dalai Lama, 81
Daly, Sara, 84–88
Darfur, Sudan, 28
Data-sharing agreements, EU-US,
  68, 71–73, 76
Davis, Raymond, 154
Dawoodzai, Omar, 146
de Maizière, Thomas, 109–110
de Oliveira, Vitória Peres, 43–50

de Vries, Gijs, 74–75
Death penalty, 71
Definitions of terrorism, 68, 69,
  73, 79, 86
Democratic demonstrations
  China, 80–81
  Muslim world, 159, 165, 168
Democratic societies, workings
  citizens' rights, 53, 57, 63–64
  India, 113, 115
  ineffective against terrorism,
    122
  Norway, 96, 98, 99, 101
Deportation
  cases, Europe, 55–56, 69
  UK policies, 59–61, 63
  US policies, 66
  See also Rendition policies
Detention without trial
  international laws, 55–56
  UK policies, 56–57, 60, 98–99,
    101
  US policies, 67, 75
Devetak, Richard, 33
Discrimination, ethnic, 82
Domino theory, 33
Doval, Ajit, 113–119
Downer, Alexander, 16
Dürbin, Tolga, 70

E

East Turkestan Islamic Movement
  (ETIM), 79, 80
Economic power shifts, global,
  148, 152
Ecuador, 45
Education
  needs, for Western world, 166,
    167–170

needs, poor and war-torn nations, 21
women's, 89, 91, 92–93
Edwards, Frances L., 100
Edwards, John, 20, 21–23
Eikenberry, Karl, 147
Elections
India and Bangladesh, 115, 118
Israel, 131
United States, primary, 20, 21–23
Ending the war on terror
death of bin Laden is not the end, 141–147
declaring victory, 148–152
Energy resources, 160
Ethnic minorities, China, 78, 82
Europe, 66–77
Charter of Fundamental Rights, 71
focus on human rights has hampered US War on Terror, 66–77
human rights laws, 53, 54–55, 62, 70–71
terrorist attacks, 68–70, 77
in West, bin Laden's death should not be excuse for racism/hate, 166–170
West must do more to end jihad-inciting injustice, 157–161
European Arrest Warrant (EAW) program, 69
European Convention on Human Rights, 54–55, 64, 71
European Council, 68, 75
European Court of Human Rights, 55, 60, 62, 63
European Police Office (Europol), 69, 73
Executions, terrorists, 87

Extremism, religious. *See* Christian fundamentalist terrorism; Islamic extremism

F

Failed states
cause terrorism, 24–29
do not cause terrorism, 30–36
as safe havens, 34–35
scholarly studies, 33
Fatah, 40, 133
Federally Administered Tribal Areas (Pakistan), 25
Financial assistance, religions, 47–48
Fisk, Robert, 97
Foreign terrorist organization (FTO) lists, 73–74, 76
Four Lions (Morris), 99
Frattini, Franco, 75–76
Full-body scanners, 106–112
Funding and financing
freezing terrorist assets, 67, 68, 73
Hezbollah, 67–68, 73–74
narcotics profits, 118
al-Qaeda, 32
tracking terrorist assets, 68, 73, 151

G

Gaddafi, Muammar, 169
Gaza
Israeli occupation, 131–132
political leadership, 40, 133
Germany, 106–112
Gillard, Julia, 16, 17
Global poverty, 20–23
Goldstein, Baruch, 135
Gonzales, Alberto, 75
Gordon, Philip H., 150

Greener-Barcham, Beth, 33

Greenfield, Daniel, 37–42

Guantánamo Bay detention facility, 71, 75, 80

Gulf War, background, 39

Guyana, 44, 45

H

Habeas corpus rights, 98–99

Haiti, 45

Halliday, F., 31

Hamas, 40, 132–133, 135

"Hambali," 87

Han Chinese, 82

Hanania, Ray, 166–170

Haq, Huda bin Abdul, 87

Haq, Zia, 157–161

Hate speech, 166, 167

Health care initiatives, global, 22–23

Hekmatyar, Gulbuddin, 144, 146

Hellwig, Tineke, 87

Hezb-e-Islami (radical Islamist group), 144

Hezbollah, 66, 67–68, 74, 76

Historical injustice roots. *See* Injustice causes of terrorism

Hitler, Adolf, 41

Hobbes, Thomas, 161

Hoffmann, Lord, 56–57

Hope, Lord, 63

House of Commons (UK), 60

House of Lords (UK), 56–58, 59, 60, 61, 62

House of Saud (Saudi Arabia), 39

Howard, John, 15

Human rights

    activists, counteracting terrorist recruiting, 91–92

    Chinese repression of Uighur separatist movement, 78–83

    EU focus has hampered US War on Terror, 66–77

    United Kingdom, respect for rights, 53–65

    United Kingdom, suspending rights, 98–99

    United States, preserving civil rights, 150

    United States, violations, 67, 71, 74–76

Human Rights Act (United Kingdom; 1998), 53, 55, 62–63, 65

Hunt, Swanee, 91

Hussein, Saddam, 39

I

Immigrant populations

    deportation laws and court proceedings, 55, 59–61

    Latin America, 45, 46–47, 49, 50

    Norway, 98

    United Kingdom, 65

Imperialism, 27, 38

Improvised explosive devices (IEDs), 100

India, 113–119, 120–129

    economy, 152

    history, 114

    response to terrorism has been complex and effective, 113–119

    response to terrorism has been ineffectual, 120–129

    terrorist violence, 25, 115, 121–122, 124, 128, 129, 143

Indonesia

    Bali bombings, 2002, 15, 87

    terrorism host environment, 36

Information gathering. *See* Intelligence

Injustice causes of terrorism
portrayals as untruth, 37,
38–39
as vague, 164
and West's responsibilities,
157–161
Intelligence
Indian response to terrorism,
113, 115–116, 117, 118, 120,
124, 126–127, 128–129
US terror focus distorts foreign policy, 148, 150–151
US war on terror should utilize, 84–88
International cooperation in war
on terror, 119
International Criminal Court
(ICC), 71
International data sharing agreements, 68, 71–73, 76
International financial assistance,
religions, 47–48
International Maritime Bureau
(IMB), 25
International Monetary Fund, 155
Internet
hate speech toward Muslims
and Arabs, 167
new Muslims' use, 48
al-Qaeda use, 32
Interventionism, 27–28
Iran
global foreign policy hopes,
160
Hezbollah as proxy, 74
Iraq War (2003–2011)
Australian troops and involve-
ment, 14, 15, 16
US instigation and presence,
23, 75, 99, 149, 151, 159,
166, 168
Irish Republican Army (IRA), 101
Isamuddin, Riduan, 87

Iskandar, Abdullah, 162–165
Islam
cause of terrorism, 37–42
de-linking from terror concept, India, 114–116
distinctness of communities,
48
not linked to terrorism in
Latin America, 43–50
peace values, 91
terrorism as opposed to, 157
Western education needs, 169
See also Muslim populations
Islamic Caliphate, 39
Islamic extremism
causes, 157, 158
European counterterrorism
priorities, 70–71
groups' actions and power,
86–88, 142, 143–144, 157–
159, 162–164, 163–164
political participation, 40
terrorist activity, Israel-
Palestine, 131, 135, 137
US counterterrorism priorities, 31, 86–88, 149–151
Wahhabism, 48
women's efforts against, 89,
90–93
Islamic holy sites, 39
Islamic Movement of Uzbekistan,
80
Islamophobia, 70, 166–170
Israel, 130–138
Hezbollah, as Iranian terrorist
proxy, 74
peace influence and importance, 159, 160, 169–170
peace negotiations with Palestine mustn't be derailed by
terrorism, 130–138
US alliance, 160, 164

J

Jamaat-u-Dawa (terrorist group), 143
Jammu, India, 115, 117, 121–122
Japan-China War (1937–1945), 41
Jarvis, Darryl S.L., 16
Jemaah Islamiyah (terrorist group), 87
Jenkins, Brian, 149–150
Jihadism, 159, 161
    Muslim world must do more to reject, 162–165
    in Pakistan, 26, 29, 90, 122
    al-Qaeda, 32, 142, 157, 158–159, 160
    West must do more to end injustice causes, 157–161
Joint Committee on Human Rights, 60
Jones, Terry, 167
Judaism tenets, 40
Judicial review, 54–55, 57

K

Kabir, Maulavi Abdul, 144
Kagan, Robert, 28
Kargil crisis (1999; India-Pakistan), 128
Karzai, Hamid, 143–144, 146
Kashmir, 115–116, 117, 121–122, 143, 160
Kenya, 36
Khobar Towers bombing (Saudi Arabia; 1996), 74
Kinsley, Michael, 122
Koran
    advocates violence, 37
    burning, 167
    terrorist interpretations, 92
Kosovo, 27

Kuwait, 39, 48
Kyrgyzstan, 79, 80

L

Laden, Osama bin
    death, 141–147, 148, 149, 151, 154, 157, 158, 166–170, 169
    hunt for, 76, 99, 144, 148–149, 151, 169
    leadership/influence, 42, 142, 157, 158–159, 160, 162–165, 167
    tribal conflict, 39, 41
Lashkar-e-Taiba, 25
Latham, Mark, 15
Latin America, 43–50
Law enforcement, local
    Germany, 110, 111
    importance in counterterrorism, 84, 86, 87–88
    India, 113, 115–116, 120, 124–127
    Norway, 100–101
    population and area ratios, 125
    Russia, 103, 104
Lawlessness, 35–36
Lebanon, 28
Lebanon, terrorism, 74
Leutheusser-Schnarrenberger, Sabine, 112
Levitt, Matthew, 130–138
Libya, 168, 169
Lisbon Treaty (2009), 71, 145
Locke, John, 161
London transportation system bombings, 2005, 68, 69–70, 96, 98–99, 100
The Looming Tower: Al-Qaeda and the Road to 9/11 (Wright), 158

M

Macwhirter, Iain, 96–101
Madrid, Spain, terrorist attacks, 2004, 68, 69
Margarita Island, 49
Masri, Abu Hamza al-, 70
McNamara, Sally, 66–77
Media influence, US, 167–168, 169
Medvedev, Dmitry, 104, 105
Menkhaus, Ken, 33, 35–36
Merkel, Angela, 70
Mexico, 45, 46
Michel, Rolf, 110–111
Middle East peace process, 42, 130–138
Militant Islam. *See* Islamic extremism
Military force
   incorrect way to fight war on terror, 84–88
   India's response has been ineffectual, 120, 127–128
   international troop strength comparisons, 126, 127
   police used for counterterrorism instead, India, 113, 115–116
   US global presence, 160
Moderate Muslims, 40
Mohammadi, Bismillah Khan, 144
Mohammed (prophet), 38–39, 41
Mongolia, 79, 80, 81
Morris, Chris, 99
Moscow suicide bombings, 2010, 102, 103, 104
Mothers, influence, 90–91, 92
Mueller, John, 149
"Mukhlas," 87
Mullah Omar, 142, 144, 146
Mumbai, India, terrorist attacks, 2008, 124, 128, 129

Murdoch, Rupert, 101
Musharraf, Pervez, 118, 144
Muslim populations
   China, and separatist repression, 78–83
   democratic uprisings, 159, 165, 168
   Europe, 70
   ignorance about, 166, 167–170
   India, 114–116, 119
   Islamophobia and anti-Muslim rhetoric, 70, 166–170
   Latin America, 43–50
   moderates, 40
   must do more to reject jihad, 162–165
   philanthropy, 167–168
   Sunni/Shia breakdown, 44

N

Narcotics profits, funding terrorism, 118
Nasrallah, Hasan, 41, 74
National Security Agency (NSA), 150, 151
National security policies
   Australia, 15, 16
   British, post-9/11, 56–57, 98–99, 101
   Germany, 109–110
   India, 113–114, 116–117, 123–125
   within peace processes, 133–134, 137–138
   poverty and national security, 21–22
   Russia, 102, 103
   United States, 21–22, 34, 107
NATO (North Atlantic Treaty Organization)
   Afghanistan conflict, 25, 28, 145

Balkans conflicts interventions, 27

International Security Assistance Force, in Pakistan, 154, 155

Taliban relations, 147

Nature of terrorism, 86, 88, 96, 99, 121, 122, 150

Nazir, Maulvi, 147

Negotiations parameters, 134–137

Netherlands, 108

News coverage, 97–98, 99, 101

9/11. *See* September 11, 2001, terrorism attacks

North-West Frontier Province (Pakistan), 25, 118

Norway, 96–101

example of calm reaction to terrorism, 96–101

terrorist attack, 2011, 96, 97–98, 99

Nuclear technology, Pakistan, 118, 155

Nurhasyim, Amrozi bin Haji, 87

O

Oakes, Dan, 15

Obama, Barack, 145, 149

Occupied Territories, 131–132, 133

Oslo peace negotiations, 1993, 131–132, 133, 135

Ottoman Empire, 38, 41

P

Pacific Islands, 33

PAIMAN (Pakistan women's organization), 92–93

Pakistan, 24–29, 89–93, 153–156

drone attacks, 151

economic isolation feared, 153–156

failed states cause terrorism, 24–29

global nations' foreign policy, 26, 153, 160

improving women's rights aids war on terror,89–93

Kashmir, 115–116, 117, 121–122, 143, 160

national strife, 118, 145

post-bin Laden environment, 141, 142–144, 145, 146, 153

terrorism host environment, 36, 116, 117–118, 143–145, 146, 153

terrorist training, 70

Palestine, 130–138

peace influence and importance, 159, 160, 169–170

peace process with Israel mustn't be derailed by terrorism, 130–138

persecution, 164

political struggles, 40, 132–133, 137

See also Arafat, Yasser

Palestinian Authority (PA), 40, 132, 133, 137

Panchen Lama, 81

Paraguay, 49

Passenger Name Record (PNR) data-sharing agreement, 68, 71–73, 76

Patrick, Stewart, 33

Peace activism, 89, 91–93, 168, 169–170

Peace process, Israel-Palestine, 42, 130–138, 159

Peace visions, 136–137, 166

Peacekeeping missions
as effective, 30
as ineffective, 28

Peres, Shimon, 131

Persian Gulf War, background, 39

Peshawar, Pakistan, 90–91, 92–93

Petraeus, David, 151

Philippines, 36

Phillips, Lord, 53–65

Phillips, Melanie, 97
Piracy, 24, 25–26, 29
Police forces, local. *See* Law enforcement, local
Poverty, global, 20–23
Pre-negotiation, peace processes, 134–137
Prevention of Terrorism Act (United Kingdom; 2005), 58
Price, Lance, 101
Prisoner rights, 75
Privacy rights
    body scanners, 107–108, 111–112
    financial data, 73
    international passenger data, 72–73
Propaganda, 41–42, 78, 82–83

Q

Qadeem, Mossarat, 89, 91–93
al-Qaeda
    Afghanistan conflict, 14, 145, 163
    bin Laden history, 142, 158–159
    counterterrorism priority, 31, 99, 149, 151
    distinctness, 32
    global reach, 31, 159, 163–164
    London transportation bombings, 2005, 68, 69
    Madrid train bombings, 2004, 68, 69
    methods, 86–88
    post-bin Laden, 146, 158–159, 162–165
    power in Pakistan, 25, 118, 141, 145, 146, 147
    See also September 11, 2001, terrorism attacks
Qaradawi, Sheikh Yusuf al-, 70
Quadrennial Defense Review (QDR; Department of Defense), 31

Qu'ran
    advocates violence, 37
    burning, 167
    terrorist interpretations, 92

R

Rachman, Gideon, 148–152
Racism, 70, 166–170
Radio waves and x-rays, 110–111
Ramer, Holly, 20–23
Reason, 161
Recruitment, terrorists
    as criminal offense, 69
    "homegrown" terrorists, 70
    al-Qaeda, 32
    Taliban, 90, 91, 92, 118
Re-education, terrorist recruits, 91
Refugees
    Pakistan, 27, 90
    UK, 65
Religious converts, Latin America, 43, 45–46, 47, 50
Religious extremism. *See* Christian fundamentalist terrorism; Islamic extremism
Rendition policies, 67, 71, 74–75
    See also Deportation
Repression, in state responses to terror
    China, 78–83
    desired by terrorists, 99
    Russia, 102, 105
    United Kingdom, 96, 98–99, 101
Rice, Condoleezza, 75
Ross, Ken, 33
Roy, Sergei, 102–105
Rudd, Kevin, 14, 16
Rule of law, failure. *See* Failed states
Russia, 102–105
    Moscow terrorist bombings, 2010, 102, 103, 104

struggles to find correct response to terrorism,102–105
Russian Federal Security Service (FSB), 103, 104
Rwanda, 28

S

Sadr, Muqata al, 41
Sahni, Ajai, 120–129
Saleh, Amrullah, 144
Samudra, Imam, 87
Saudi Arabia
　bin Laden relations, 39
　Hussein relations, 39
　political assassinations, 111
　al-Qaeda history, 31
　terrorist attacks, 74
　Wahhabi Islam, 48
Schaar, Peter, 112
Schäuble, Wolfgang, 109–110
Schemann, Serge, 131
Scheuer, Michael, 160
Second Intifada, 132
Sennott, Charles M., 89–93
Separatist movements
　China, suppression, 78–83
　India, 117
September 11, 2001, terrorism attacks
　books about, 158
　causes, 15, 158, 160
　effects on Australia, 14
　effects on British human rights policy, 56
　effects on Chinese domestic policy, 78, 79–80
　European counterterrorism following, 67, 68–69, 71
　European counterterrorism preceding, 68
　al-Qaeda, 32, 99
　US counterterrorism and foreign policy following, 99, 149–152

Settlements, Israeli, 131–132
Sheikh, Abdul Hafeez, 153, 154–155
Shia Islam, 44
Singh, Manmohan, 123–124
Sino-Japanese War (second; 1937–1945), 41
Sipah-e-Sahaba (terrorist group), 143
Social inclusion and exclusion, 46
Social media, 167
Social recruitment methods, 32
Socialist nations, 39
Society for Worldwide Interbank Financial Telecommunication, 68, 73
Somalia, 24–29, 30–36
　failed states cause terrorism,24–29
　failed states do not cause terrorism,30–36
　piracy, 25–26, 29
　US presence and intelligence, 28, 34–35, 149
Spain, terrorist attacks, 2004, 68, 69
Special Immigration Appeals Commission (United Kingdom), 59–61
"Special Operations" Army forces, 34, 35
Speeches, leaders, 42
Der Spiegel, 106–112
State repression. *See* Repression, in state responses to terror
Steinhäusler, Friedrich, 100
Stoltenberg, Jens, 98
Strip searches, 106, 107–108
Sudan
　Darfur conflict, 28
　al-Qaeda in, 32
Suicide bombers
　London, England terrorism, 68

Moscow, Russia terrorism, 102, 103, 104
portrayals, 99
recruiting, Pakistan, 90, 92
Sunni Islam
  as Muslim majority, 44
  Wahhabism, 48
Supreme Courts
  India, 126
  United Kingdom, 53, 54, 59, 62, 63
Suriname, 44, 45

T

Tabloid news coverage, 101
Tagliacozzo, Eric, 87
Taliban, 80, 163
  Afghanistan relations, 141, 143, 145, 146
  locals' efforts against, 89, 90–93
  power in Pakistan, 25, 27, 90, 93, 118, 141, 142–143, 144, 146, 147
  US efforts against, 145, 146, 147
Tax policies, United States, 22–23
Terrorism Act (UK; 2000), 71
Terrorist screening, 72–73, 106–112
Terrorist watch lists, 67, 68
Thatcher, Margaret, 101
"Three Evils," 81–82
Tibet, 81, 82, 83
Torture
  human rights protection from, 53, 55, 67
  US policies, 67, 75–76
Training, terrorists
  camps, 70
  as criminal offense, 69
  "homegrown" terrorists, 70
  al-Qaeda methods and manuals, 32

Transportation security policies
  aviation, 106–112, 116
  customs, 108
  Passenger Name Record (PNR) data-sharing agreement, 68, 71–73, 76
Tribal conflicts, 38–40, 41
Trinidad and Tobago, 44, 45

U

Uighur separatist movement, China, 78–83
UK, A. v. (1998), 60
"Underwear bomber" terrorism attempt, 2009, 106, 107, 108, *109,* 112
United Kingdom, 53–65, 96–101
  antiterrorism laws and strategy, 56–58, 60, 63, 68–69, 71, 98–99
  respect for human rights,53–65
  should learn to react calmly to attacks, 96–101
  terrorism history, 101
  terrorist attacks, 2005, 68, 69–70, 96, 98–99, 100, 101
  US ally, 67
United Kingdom, Chahal v. (1996), 55
United Nations (UN)
  Arafat address, 1974, 42
  on counterterrorism, 160–161
  members killed, 167
  peacekeeping missions and challenges, 28
  piracy policy, 26
  Universal Declaration of Human Rights, 1948, 64
United States, 20–23, 84–88, 148–152
  Afghanistan foreign policy, 141, 146–147, 149, 151, 166, 168
  bin Laden target, 160, 167

economy, 20, 22–23, 148, 152
EU focus on human rights
has hampered war on terror,
66–77
global military presence, 160
human rights violations, 67,
71, 74–76
interventionism and foreign
policy, 28
Iraq foreign policy, 23, 75, 99,
149, 151, 159, 166, 168
Pakistan foreign policy, 26, 29,
141, 153–156
piracy policy, 26
post-war on terror society,
150
should declare victory and
end war on terror, 148–152
should fight global poverty to
reduce terrorism,20–23
war on terror should utilize
intelligence, not military,
84–88
in West, bin Laden's death
should not be excuse for
racism/hate, 166–170
West must do more to end
jihad-inciting injustice, 157–
161
world standing diminished, 75
See also September 11, 2001,
terrorism attacks
Universal Declaration of Human
Rights (1948), 64
US Army, Civil Affairs & Psychological Operations Command,
34, 35
US Department of Defense, Quadrennial Defense Review (QDR),
31

US Embassies bombings, 74
US National Security Strategy, 34

V

Van Rompuy, Herman, 76

W

Wahhabi Islam, 48
Wardak, Abdul Rahim, 144
Washington, D.C., 150
Washington Post, 150, 151
Water and sanitation, 22
"The West." *See* Europe; United
States
West Bank, 131–132, 133
Williams, Paul D., 30–36
Women's work against terrorism,
89, 90–93
World Bank, 155
Wright, Lawrence, 158

X

Xinjiang, China, 79, 80–81, 83
X-rays, 110–111

Y

Yemen
pirate attacks, 25
terrorism host environment,
36, 149, 158

Z

Zawahiri, Ayman al-, 163